UN-TRAIN
YOUR
BRAIN

UN-TRAIN YOUR BRAIN

A FORMULA FOR FREEDOM
(FROM THE NEURONS THAT HOLD YOU BACK)

MIKE WEEKS

Vermilion
LONDON

1 3 5 7 9 10 8 6 4 2

Vermilion, an imprint of Ebury Publishing,
20 Vauxhall Bridge Road,
London SW1V 2SA

Vermilion is part of the Penguin Random House group of companies
whose addresses can be found at global.penguinrandomhouse.com

Penguin
Random House
UK

First published by Vermilion in 2016

www.eburypublishing.co.uk

A CIP catalogue record for this book is available from the British Library

ISBN 9781785040115

Printed and bound in Great Britain by Clays Ltd, St Ives PLC

| MIX |
| Paper from responsible sources |
| FSC   FSC® C018179 |
| www.fsc.org |

Penguin Random House is committed to a
sustainable future for our business, our readers
and our planet. This book is made from Forest
Stewardship Council® certified paper.

DEDICATION

For Bean and our boys, and the spontaneous joy, laughter and love you each bring.

In writing this book my intention is to share with readers a number of the transformational 'Patterns' that I have been lucky enough to learn and use in my personal life as well as my work as a trainer and coach.

Much of what I present in this book I have learned from my mentors, Carmen Bostic St. Clair and John Grinder, two of the world's geniuses who continue to model and code patterns of 'excellence' so that people like you and I can become better at everything we do.

I am indebted to you both for a decade of training me how to operate my own brain, which began before I gave much thought to having a brain at all!

CONTENTS

ABOUT THIS BOOK

Some books ask the question, 'Why do we humans do what we do?' This book asks, 'How do we do what we do?' and specifically, 'How is it that we often think and act in ways that we would prefer not to?' Most importantly, this book tells you how you can swap those unwanted thoughts and behaviours for new ones that will serve you better.

By practising the outlined steps (patterns) in this book you will begin to change your brain and nervous system to have freedom to think, feel and behave how you want to. This could be as varied as a child losing their fear of the dark, a business CEO communicating less aggressively with his colleagues, or it could be a performer overcoming stage fright or a commuter learning to deal with his anger and frustration at being in yet another traffic jam. Or it could be a person who already has a great life but who wants to help others too.

Regardless of what current thoughts and behaviours hold you back, by applying what you learn in the following chapters you will be able to make positive changes in all areas of your life.

Using these same methods, I have helped countless people create the freedom to live without negative emotions and the bad habits that can sabotage their dreams. My intention is that by the end of this book you will be able to do the same.

This book has been written for, and about, our two minds, the conscious and the unconscious. In each chapter you will read a number of stories (and anecdotes) that come from my work with my own clients. These stories are written to provide meaning at a different level of understanding from the explicit descriptions. Therefore there is no need to consciously 'understand' these stories. Simply read them and allow yourself to experience the meaning in different forms.

Each chapter also contains one or more 'pattern(s)'. These are series of steps to focus your attention on. Unlike the stories, these patterns require your full attention. When they are applied to your life they will lead you towards a positive shift in the way you perceive, feel, behave and communicate. I highly encourage you to use and practise each pattern until it becomes second nature to you. To make the experience of following these patterns more thorough and enjoyable, I have provided accompanying video and audio tutorials in website and app form at: www.untrainyourbrain.com

If you have a smartphone you can download (from your app store) a Quick Response Code (QR Code) reader and scan each exercise to be viewed or listened to on your device. See page 235 for a list of specific URLs used in the book.

NB You may find it helpful and useful to start a small diary or journal to make notes of your progress and write about any of the exercises. Alternatively there is space to write in the book itself, if that suits you better.

ABOUT THE AUTHOR

Mike Weeks is an international trainer and coach. He teaches and troubleshoots in locations as diverse as the slums of Haiti and the boardrooms of London. His unique style for creating change has been seen on TV shows in over 150 countries.

For further information see www.untrainyourbrain.com and www.mikeweeks.co

ESSENTIAL TERMS

Over a decade ago, when I first started learning the 'patterns' I write about in this book, I sat at the back of a class and asked, 'Huh, "patterns?" What on earth does that mean in regard to change methods?' In fact, during my first week of being taught the very basics of what you will learn in this book, I had such a limited vocabulary that I missed huge amounts of important teaching points, simply because the terms and specific language held little to no meaning for me.

As I've written this book I've made an effort to use as little jargon as I possibly can. However there are a small number of essential descriptions and terms that I have included because more commonly used words may be misinterpreted. The use of precise language is primarily important when it comes to directing the reader's attention to the steps (patterns) throughout the various exercises.

Below is a small glossary of essential terms I use. I also later repeat descriptions at the various points they are likely to be needed. Please take a few minutes to familiarise yourself with the terms – it will make your journey through these pages a smoother one.

The most effective use of the change patterns will come from first reading the descriptions in this book, followed by using the accompanying videos or audio on the Un-train Your Brain app.

The terms

Associated and **dissociated** are words to describe our relationship to a memory or present experience. When we are associated we may see, hear, smell, taste and feel as if through our own senses. When we are dissociated, we are detached from the experience and can even view our whole body in a memory as an outside observer would. A full dissociation could be called an 'out-of-body' view of ourselves, though in this book it bears no relation to the alleged after-death experience of the same name.

Calibration refers to the measuring of our own, and other people's, states. Humans have a capacity for matching observed emotional states from one person to another and will often say that a person looks 'happy', 'sad', 'peaceful', 'upset', etc.

To get the most out of this book I recommend avoiding these forms of labelling and instead learning to calibrate what can be observed or heard in the other person and yourself without rushing to attach an emotional label to it. As an example of self-calibration, you might bring your attention to your body sensations and at a particular point in time, say that you have tightness in your chest, your jaw is clenched and your hands are squeezing as you notice that your voice goes up in pitch when speaking. Some people might call this state 'stressed', but I ask you only to notice what you see, hear and feel rather than applying a label.

When calibrating to another person you might see that he/she has a relaxed face, steady, slow breathing and loose shoulders with a soft voice tone. You might call this state 'calm' and again I ask that you only notice what you can see and hear and not try to interpret the state. The reason for this non-labelling will become clear later in the book.

Choice in this book is not about the colour or styles of new clothing, or what you will eat from a menu. It relates to our ability to have multiple and, ultimately, infinite degrees of options available in how we respond to the world around us. As one of an infinite number of examples, a person who is given feedback on their behaviour may react by becoming aggressively defensive without knowing why or what to do about it. This is an absence of behavioural choice as the reaction happens to the person against their conscious intent or wishes.

However, another person who receives precisely the same feedback and yet chooses how to respond in such a case has choice. When we react in ways that create undesirable consequences, or when we exhibit patterns of behaviour that we're unaware of, but are told by others that they are questionable or inappropriate, we are without choice.

Congruent, congruence and **congruency** refer to a state of harmony of unconscious and conscious processing or mind. When someone presents as being aligned in their words, actions and body language, they are congruent. The opposite, **incongruent**, is a conflict between how you feel and how you present yourself. As an example, when you meet someone you genuinely love, your response will be congruent. When you meet someone you dislike but decide to be polite towards, you are likely being incongruent.

Context is what we see, hear and experience around us to form the setting and fuller understanding of an event, relationship or idea. If I say that a young woman is screaming at the top of her lungs and I do not provide a context, the reader will likely make certain assumptions (perhaps that she is being attacked). If I provide contextual information that the woman is on holiday and riding a roller coaster (and is enjoying herself), the event changes in character and meaning.

Filters, in this book, are a way to describe how we each organise incoming information from our world. Humans tend to acquire filters from the cultures we inhabit. For example, an Inuit will have multiple ways of viewing (perception filters) the use of snow, whereas a desert-living Berber will likely only view snow as one thing.

It's useful to be able to use multiple perceptual filters and adjust or create new ones. To do so enables the user to receive a broader range and quality of information about the world.

Freedom from the neurons that hold us back, refers to our capability to think, act and live as we really want to. This is the opposite of living with perceived limits, fears, bad habits/patterns and cultural influences dictating our actions.

Hallucination is the experience of sensing something that does not presently exist in the moment. If I point to an empty space and invite a person to see a piece of fruit or a small animal, he or she is often able to get a vague sense of such an object being in that empty space. If I ask you to recall one of your parents calling your name when you were a child, you're likely to 'hear' that voice to some degree, despite the fact that the voice belongs in the past.

Take a moment now to hallucinate a lemon and then, with it firmly in your hand, take a big juicy bite out of it. Does it hit your senses, despite its absence in the real world? This is hallucination. I use this word throughout the book instead of words like 'imagine', in part because I've heard many people tell me that they have no imagination at all. Being able to hallucinate, even a little bit, will be really useful for getting the most out of the patterns in this book.

Neurons are the cells in our body that process and transmit information through electrical and chemical signals and that are the important components of our brain, spinal cord and nervous system.

Neurology refers to the entire operating system of brain, spinal cord and connecting nerves. To varying degrees, everything we do engages the whole person and not just compartmentalised areas of our brain or spinal cord. When you engage with the patterns in this book you will do so while using your whole neurology.

Patterns, when connected to behaviours, are those that we repeat in a sequence that is reliably predictable. As an example, a person may start a new diet every January, only to give it up a month later and then diet again before the summer holidays, after which they give up dieting for the winter. The pattern becomes a predictable one each year: dieting followed by weight gain. On a smaller scale, most of us clean our teeth in the same way, speak to our partners about similar things, sit in the same chairs, wear our favourite clothes, drive the same route to work, check our phone at regular intervals and use and engage in a multitude of regular habitual activities. Patterns are these regular, and often predictable, sequences of how we go about life.

I also use the word **pattern** to describe the precise sequence of steps in each chapter that is intended to focus your attention. These steps are provided to guide you to an intended change in your 'state' and behaviour. The steps carried out in a certain order create the pattern.

Perceptual positions: When we perceive through our senses we mostly do so as ourselves, in a First Position of our own experience of seeing, hearing, tasting, feeling and smelling. In this book you will learn how to expand your perception into positions other than your self. You will learn Second Position, which is an ability to experience the world through the senses of another person, as well as learning a Third Position, which is the ability to view our self and others as an observer who is free of any of the states (feelings) that may arise when in the First or Second Positions.

Resourcefulness and **resourceful states** are when we experience clever and effective ways to overcome problems, challenges and difficulties.

State is the condition and feelings that we experience in our physiology, neurology and biochemistry (everything involved in who and what we are) at any given time. We express ourselves (through behaviour) as a consequence of the states we experience and often use commonly agreed upon labels to describe these feelings that we all broadly share. These state labels include 'happy', 'sad', 'hungry', 'tired', 'depressed', 'excited', 'lonely', etc.

What is important to appreciate is that though we may agree on the names of these commonly experienced feelings, the actual sensations that any two or more people may be experiencing are often different. This is why I do not over-use the emotional labels: 'happy', 'sad', 'angry', 'depressed', etc, in this book and instead refer to what we experience as ' state', so that you, the reader, can add your own understanding of what it is you are feeling.

INTRODUCTION

'There is only one corner of the universe you can be certain of improving, and that's your own self.'

Aldous Huxley

When a young captive elephant is separated from its mother and prepared for training, maybe in the circus or as an animal for transport, heavy chains are attached to it and fixed to posts driven deep into the ground. At first the young elephant pulls, strains and struggles against his captivity, but the chains and fixings are too strong and the animal tires.

Eventually, the animal gives up and learns to accept his leashed status, now believing that he is incapable of breaking free. From this moment on, the trainers can attach the animal by a thin rope that the elephant accepts as being unbreakable. Even as the elephant grows strong enough to snap chains with ease, this huge being stops attempting to change his situation and simply accepts it as reality.

When I offer this metaphor in my seminars and training events, I usually get a nodding of heads in approval and recognition at what the story is pointing at. On a rare occasion when a trainee is really paying attention, I will be asked or challenged over the elephant's conditioned response:

Trainee: 'But what happens if something provokes the elephant into trying again, or it gets scared and runs, pulling its cord out of the ground one more time?'

Mike: 'The elephant disproves what it believed was true about its own condition, and then the game is up and the elephant is hightailing it to freedom.'

1

This book is about how people allow themselves to be leashed by a number of limiting and unhelpful ideas, beliefs and learned reactions, and, more importantly, how each of us can slip that leash and experience freedom.

Freedom, as presented here, is achieved by creating new ways of thinking and behaving where we previously thought and behaved in ways that were unhelpful and limiting to both ourselves and to others. This means knowing how to have choice in how we respond to the world around us at all times. You can learn to do this by focusing your attention and actions in specific ways that you will learn throughout this book.

There are institutions, therapeutic fields and guru figures that would have us all believe that our lives are governed by our past, or perhaps the current environments we find ourselves in, or even by the hand of unseen forces. Worse still are the dangerous assumptions that who we are and how we operate in the world are fixed, to a greater degree, and that our thoughts, feelings and behaviours happen to us rather than it being us who are creating those experiences.

What I invite you to consider at this beginning stage is that all of us have the availability of choice over our thoughts, feelings and behaviours, regardless of how good or bad the outer world may be.

What does this form of choice look like? View yourself in an emergency of some kind and everyone around you is panicking. Having choice in this instance means that you know how to adjust your feelings, or more specifically, your 'state' and can therefore respond calmly instead of just reacting and panicking like everyone else. Or perhaps you are asked to make an impromptu speech, which triggers a release of adrenaline and nervous energy. With the ability to choose how you feel you can reduce your nerves and access a confident and resourceful state from which you are able to recall any number of compelling and funny stories. Or maybe your young child has been up all night and you and your partner are exhausted, sleep-deprived and bickering the next day over the small stuff. Using the methods in this book you can quickly step into your partner's shoes long enough to appreciate how they too are doing their best while struggling to keep their eyes open, just like you. Maybe you are a high-level performer of some kind who is in the spotlight for a once-in-a-lifetime act of brilliance. This is your moment – as you shift all of your doubt and fear and instead choose a high-performance state from which to display complete mastery and brilliance. Or you have responsibilities and a job you do not enjoy. Instead of running on what feels like a hamster wheel and getting nowhere, you can simply take five minutes out and clearly observe your situation, which enables you to then create compelling and workable solutions to the predicament you find yourself in.

Many people have some fairly obvious patterns of behaviour running throughout their lives. From what you might call procrastination or confusion, worry or boredom, stress and anger, we can often find ourselves reacting to events in predictable ways every time and getting a repeat of unwanted results again and again. The challenge for some people is that they are a little too much like the elephant and failing to test their own beliefs about what really holds them back.

So how do we know if we are living a life of our own choosing, rather than a conditioned response like the elephant?

The following questions may help you assess that answer (there is no score, simply answer with 'yes' or 'no'):

- Do you get out of bed in the morning to a day mostly containing activities you would prefer not to be undertaking?
- Do you wake up next to a person you would rather not wake up next to?
- Do you wake up alone when you wish you had someone there with you?
- Do you wake up to label your feelings as sad, depressed, angry, lonely or fearful?
- Do you wake up in a location that you do not like?
- Do you eat a breakfast you do not enjoy?

- Do you work in a role or a business you find meaningless?
- Do you remain jobless when you really want to work?
- Do you work only for money?
- Do you commute while you would prefer not to?
- Do you work from home but wish you had an office to travel to?
- Do you remain silent on your commute because you are too self-conscious to speak to others?
- Do you feel dread or misery as you walk into your workplace?
- Do you drop into patterns of un-useful thinking, eating, working and interacting throughout your day?
- Do you dream of more but do nothing about it?
- Do you have relationships in which you experience tension, anger, distrust or dislike?
- Do you experience easily preventable health problems?
- Do you experience unexplainable ill health and resent it?
- Do you rely upon tobacco, alcohol, drugs, food, porn, gambling and other stimulants to amplify your feelings?
- Do you often buy things you do not need?
- Do you hurt other people intentionally or unintentionally and later regret it?
- Do you hurt yourself emotionally or physically and not regret it?
- Do you fear being punished by a force or being that is taking account of your every wrong move and expecting you to obey rules from an ancient and out-of-date world?
- Do you believe in luck as a deciding factor in your life?
- Do you blame others for outcomes that you could influence in some way?
- Do you blame others for any aspect of your own life?
- Do you sleep badly?
- Do you sleep too much?
- Do you fear living the life of your dreams?
- Do you fear events that you could prevent?
- Do you fail at activities, only to give up on them?
- Do you avoid activities for fear of failing?
- Do you use your mobile phone or computer to avoid having face-to-face interactions?

- Do you check your phone regularly in the hope of being messaged or receiving likes to your social media posts?
- Do you abhor, hate, loathe, envy, fear, covet, mourn, pity or resent others for long enough periods that you feel the experience affects your health?

If you answered 'yes' to any of these questions this is an example of where and how you could benefit from more choice and freedom over your own thoughts and behaviours.

Any neurons that might be holding you back are actually little cells that receive and transmit information throughout the nervous system while connecting to many millions of other neurons. They aren't static but rather living, with the capacity to change over time. The more we send signals between different neurons the stronger the connections grow and so with each new experience that we have, our brain and nervous system changes in some small way.

Rather than reinforcing the connections that we experience as unwanted thoughts, states and behaviours, we can instead shift our attention to new experiences that will then positively change what we do.

One of the first steps to building these new connections is to realise that the world we know for ourselves is not the absolute world, but more of a convenient version of our own making. As an example of this, consider how different the world you live in would look to a member of a remote Amazonian tribe? Or how different clouds must look to a child and a meteorologist? How different the ocean is to a sailor and an Arab born in the Sahara desert? What about the information that sound holds for a fully sighted person compared to someone who is blind?

All of us are trained to experience the world as something very different from what it actually is and when we begin to grasp the subjective nature of our experiences, we can open ourselves to a multitude of possibilities that were previously invisible to us. This includes what we perceive to be true about ourselves and what we are ultimately capable of.

Acquiring the clarity to see that life, including ourselves, is more than we believe it to be, may well be the ultimate form of freedom, as the poet, William Blake, wrote:

'To see a World in a Grain of Sand

And a Heaven in a Wild Flower,

Hold Infinity in the palm of your hand

And Eternity in an hour.'

CHAPTER 1

FREEDOM FROM WHAT?

The brain has specific areas that enable us to copy behaviours from our earliest of ages. This process of learning influences who we are as adults, but is in no way a valid reason to accept our own perceived limitations. If we want to change and become all we can be, it is better to take responsibility for our lives and not use the past as an excuse for our actions in the present.

> 'If you do not change direction, you may end up where you are heading.'
>
> Lao Tzu

What is it that you are *doing* right now that you really want to change?

There are a number of ways to ask this important question and the answers that come back often tend to be vague or even confused. Many people whom I work with in my coaching practice assume that life is something that is happening *to* them rather than created *by* them and their actions. The 'what are you doing?' part of the question confuses people most when they have come to me for emotional issues that they believe they have no control over. 'I don't control my problems', said one lady, 'they control me'.

I disagree, and by the end of this book you will understand why.

Un-train ...

When I first began learning and applying the methods I am teaching now, I was more than a little sceptical. Back when I first started coaching people, I would hear from experienced practitioners that the commonly stated emotions: anxiety, fear, panic, anger, frustration, embarrassment, guilt, sadness, depression, low self-esteem and procrastination could all be shifted seemingly magically within minutes and hours rather than within weeks and months. At first, this quick-fix approach appealed to me at a personal level because of what was going on in my own life. The desire to help people with these methods grew much later, after I had experienced my own radical, positive changes.

As a kid, I grew up in a volatile and unstable family setting, where even the smallest of disputes was dealt with by flying off the handle and letting emotions roar forth. I left home as soon as I could drive a car and used the first opportunity to distance myself from where I had grown up. But I also knew that I carried within me feelings and reactions that could surface – or rather explode – without warning, and then influence my actions.

The idea of therapy had always repelled me, partly because I prefer jumping in to act when something needs my attention instead of simply talking about a problem. So to learn that there were practices available that might provide me with a choice over how I felt and how I behaved, regardless of the situation, sounded too good to be true.

I dedicated a large portion of my time and resources to learning as much as possible in the fields of self-development and change. I studied under a number of well-known psychologists, coaches and maverick therapists. After a couple of years I had learned a lot but achieved varying results. While there were many great ideas on offer, very little stuck with me or affected me positively over the long term. Then, in 2006, my girlfriend, now my wife, encouraged me to join her on a training programme that promised to teach methods for making changes to the unconscious part of the mind. The programme offered everything I had been looking for, not only to increase my performance in my six-day-a-week obsession of rock-climbing, but also enabling me to be more effective in my business ventures, as well as to learn how to change my emotions whenever I desired.

After some resistance and the cancelling of a long-planned rock-climbing trip, I agreed to accompany the smart person in our relationship, but with a little more scepticism than optimism. Only a few days into the training, I turned to my girlfriend and said, 'I feel like I've had my brain un-trained', which was an odd but accurate way of putting what I had just experienced. Minutes prior, I had applied one of the 'patterns' we had been taught to a feeling of grief that I had experienced all too often. My father had died tragically when I was a teenager and for many years, whenever I recalled the experience, a heavy, painful crushing sensation wrenched my chest. In line with the promise of the training, I applied what I had been taught. After only 10 minutes of playing the strange 'clapping/rhythm' game I had just learned, the unwanted feelings simply disappeared and I was unable to get them back. For the first time in 13 years I was able to recall everything about my father without feeling any of the usual sadness.

I compared that moment to my favourite scene in the movie *The Matrix*. The lead character, Neo, is offered a choice between a blue pill and a red one. The former allows him to go back to his known reality that was very cosy and comfortable but based on a lie. The latter opens the doors to an entirely unexpected world. I had swallowed the red pill. From that moment on I immersed myself in the methods I was learning and applied them to every context of my life in which I identified a need for change – and the list was long.

For many years now, I have been using these same change patterns in my work as a coach and trainer to assist people from all over the world in creating positive differences in their lives. My work brings me into contact with a diverse range of people, from elite athletes and billionaire businessmen to kids living in third-world slums and special forces' personnel who go through repeated recalls of war-time service experiences. As you would expect, the needs and desires of each person are unique. However, we all have a similar capacity to use our brains and nervous systems – or neurology – to create states and behaviours that can drive us to be motivated, focused, confident, relaxed, curious, effective and happy, or whatever you desire – as and when you choose and without the need to swallow a red pill, or any pill at all.

It's you or no one

I've met a number of people born in developing countries who have plenty of excuses not to excel and yet who go on to *create* highly successful lives. I emphasise the word 'create' because only a few of us experience the lifestyles we desire without making regular constructive actions, like walking two hours every day to and from school – as one of my young friends has done for the past three years in northern Africa. In fact, if you think about the main purpose of our neurology, its most fundamental role is to propel us into actions of all kinds.

When we look around us it's easy to see that life rarely exists in static form but rather at varying speeds of activity. The nature of living things seems to dictate that anything not evolving and growing eventually dies out. It's the same for people. Those who create the life they desire often do so because of consistent effort towards learning, improving their knowledge and skills and developing to be more effective in what they do.

A strong commitment to self-improvement is often what makes the difference between average and 'world-class' performers. By using the word 'performers', I am not singling out the sports or arts; I also mean performance in each of our ordinary day-to-day activities, from making breakfast to sending emails. It often requires the same degree of physical effort to do things well, as it does to do them badly, and who does not want to be their best in all contexts, from family and friends, career, health, finances, romances and other interests? The problem for many of us isn't the lack of desire to create a better life, it's that most of what we do is habitual and seemingly out of our grasp to change.

You again?

Over the course of our lives, most of our behaviours become repeated patterns. We sleep on, and get out of, the same side of the bed, put the same foot first into a shoe, brush our teeth with the same hand, eat the same breakfast, travel the same route to work or school, greet the same people with the same degree of enthusiasm or dread. We have our preferred dining places, our preferred clothes, our favourite chairs and we watch our preferred programmes on TV. If cameras were used for recording the majority of our activities in only a few short days we would likely observe very clear repeats of activity in every context of our lives.

Some patterns improve our lives: brushing our teeth, exercising, furthering our knowledge and spending time with our loved ones, for example. Other patterns do not serve us so well, like staying up late into the night and exhausting ourselves, going into debt, allowing ourselves to be affected by stressful situations and not brushing our teeth.

Most of our habits and what we do on a day-to-day basis run on an autopilot setting, arising from our unconscious mind, and remaining largely hidden from our moment-to-moment awareness. This lack of awareness is often highlighted in how other people view us compared to how we view ourselves. At times our best intentions can be misrepresented by our behaviours and taken to mean anything but what we want them to.

As an example, a close friend of mine is known for being stoic, distant and even 'grumpy'. When I once mentioned this to him, he looked at me in confusion and told me that I was off in my assessment. In his opinion, he was a world-class listener and the most attentive of our entire peer group. He had been harbouring something of an annoyance with most of his accusers, who, he claimed, rarely took time to fully listen and care for what was being said!

To be in the game of creating positive change in our lives, we first need to have an awareness of our own patterns, how our lives would look to an outsider, and how we might have got there.

You did what?

I invite you to take a few minutes to consider an aspect of your life that is *not* working for you. This could be in the area of your finances, relationships, health, career, or some other category. When you have the specific context in mind, ask yourself:

'What repeated thoughts, behaviours and actions am I aware of that got me to this current outcome?'

As two possible examples of many, maybe you are close to losing your job, or you have already lost it, and you can observe the actions that got you fired: turning up late, failing to meet targets, undermining your boss, assuming too much about your job security. Or perhaps a relationship failed and you can see that you chose to look at the negative behaviours of that person and did not appreciate any positives, which then led you to be overly critical and judgemental in your communication.

Make a note of the repeated thoughts and actions that you are aware of that led to one unwanted outcome – you can start your own notebook/journal to record your responses, or use space in this book.

Unwanted outcome:

Thoughts and behaviours that created it:

Now think of an aspect of your life that works for you and that you consider to represent a successful outcome. This can be on a large scale, like a business venture, or it can be what you might consider to be small, such as a friendship or skill that you have learned.

Successful outcome:

Thoughts and behaviours that created it:

If you have been honest about what actions you take, you will see that regardless of the outcome – good or bad – what brought you to your current position was a series of consistent steps, some intentional and some not. All these actions were yours to take, no matter how much you might think other people or events are responsible for what you do. As you will learn throughout this book, we always have at least some choice regarding how we respond to events that happen around us.

If you spend time with really successful individuals or groups, you will notice that they rarely, if ever, apportion blame or use excuses when they experience failure or setbacks. To be a success in our relationships, work, health, community or any aspect of our lives requires us to accept 100 per cent responsibility for any actions that have gained us failure or success.

As you will learn in Chapter 3 (Freedom from excuses), there is never a time or place in our lives when we do not have the availability of choice. Even with a literal or proverbial gun to our head, there are an infinite amount of responses available to us in each moment. This is the ability to make effective choices and be 'resourceful', meaning that we can come up with clever solutions to the problems confronting us. If you regularly use blame or excuses, you're doing the opposite of resourceful.

Of the many questions I ask clients, one that tends to provoke people the most is:

'What does it require for you to accept 100 per cent responsibility for all of your life in this very moment?'

This means that all of your decisions and actions – and only those – got you where you are, and whatever degree of success or failure you might currently be experiencing is down to you.

'Between stimulus and response, there is a space. In that space is our power to choose our response. In our response lies our growth and our freedom.'

Viktor E. Frankl, Holocaust survivor
and author of *Man's Search for Meaning*

When we take accountability for our lives, we get to create more choice, ultimately enabling us to have more direction over where we are going and ultimately the freedom to live more as we desire. For example, if we believe that our unwanted experiences in a relationship are due to something outside of our control, such as our zodiac sign or the way our parents treated us when we were young, we automatically lessen our ability to make the much-needed changes in this context. The moment we blame external conditions for our personal lives, we take away our potential to create solutions. If a bird perching on a lamp post happens to poop on your new clothes, was it not you who stood under the lamp post in the first place? And is it not you who can decide to remain there, complaining to a creature that doesn't give a sh**, or instead find the nearest bathroom to get cleaned up immediately?

But it doesn't feel like I have a choice!

When I first started working as a coach, I specialised in the field of fitness and weight loss, as this was an obvious extension of my years' training as a full-time rock-climber. I coach many people who want to acquire, or regain, good health, and one commonly shared pattern that I often encounter with overweight clients is their capacity to go long stretches of the day with very little, or no, food. This is often followed by a moment in the evening when they feel ravenously hungry and lose all 'control', to binge on high-sugar, high-carb 'reward' foods like cakes and biscuits. Not surprisingly, a mist of cravings seems to descend upon the person as all previous considerations of the consequences they wish to avoid, disappear in a pile of crumbs.

I have heard the words, 'I lose all control' all too often, not only from weight-loss clients, but also from people who tell me that all of a sudden, as if from nowhere, they experience states of anxiety and panic, phobias, stress reactions, embarrassment, fears and a range of really unwanted feelings. Yet, nobody I know rises in the morning and consciously decides that today they will have a really strong negative reaction to the world and make themselves, and others, feel bad.

These unwanted states arise unconsciously and, as you will learn in Chapter 5 (Freedom from one mind), our unconscious processing, or mind, is the main driver of our behaviours while mostly operating outside of our regular awareness. This could create something of a challenge to my proposal that we each take 100 per cent responsibility for our lives and the actions that get us there. If our actions are mostly driven by the unconscious mind, which is beyond *most* people's usual sphere of influence, then who is responsible for what we do each day?

As any person who is battling with their weight will tell you, he or she can be given all the logical advice in the world to eat a salad instead of pasta, but more often than not, the unconscious sensations we recognise as 'cravings' will drive the final choice. You may share a similar experience with some of the individuals who have told me that they feel as though they downloaded a faulty operating program, designed to sabotage their best intentions and ruin all plans for a successful life. Which, albeit not being entirely accurate, is a useful analogy for how many of our formative behaviours are acquired from the moment we come into the world.

Early learnings

Knowing how we learn in our earliest years can provide important insights into the choices we make and the actions we take as adults. It can also give us clues as to why we might react the way we do in later life, despite our best efforts not to.

The following experience brought home to me just how early in our lives we each begin to gather information from our world and use it to become who we are.

My first son came into the world at home, in the additional presence of me and two wonderful midwives, who quietly stood back, observed and allowed my wife's instincts to repeat the act that got most of us here in the world today. Within moments of his debut, the strange little alien was placed on my wife's belly and gently supported in place, with his eyes at her lower chest line. He rolled his head around and around, making little mewing noises and mouthing like a mini shark at what I assume he hoped was a milk source, but was in fact thin air.

After 30 minutes of moving and head-rolling like one of those nodding toys you see in shop windows at Christmas, our boy began to utilise some form of internal-navigation system and commenced the short crawl and wriggle a little north and then north-east. Pushing himself up and then flopping to gain a centimetre per push was the form this first adventure took. He would lift his head to stare at his mama, followed by a head flop and taste of his hands and the skin in front of him. Breathing happened mostly through his tiny little nostrils, and then his head came up again as another centimetre of ground was gained. This stare-lick-smell process went on until he found his way to the promised land, where he spent another 10 minutes assessing the territory before finally connecting with his first-ever al fresco breakfast.

One of my earliest lucid thoughts that arrived after a hundred others including, 'I don't recall other babies looking *that* odd', and, 'Wow, he's got enough hair to join the Muppet Show', was, how did he know which direction to wriggle in if no one was telling or showing him? And how did he know that a breast was the place to make for, and not the armpit or the chin?

I pondered on the idea of an inborn, genetic tracking device that could direct my son's travels, a little like a migratory bird uses to find its way back to its ancestral nesting grounds or a salmon might use to swim back up-river to spawn. Some answers came from two researchers, Klaus and Kennel, who considered this back in 1998. They came to a number of important conclusions about what is known as 'the breast crawl', which is when a mother places a newborn on her belly and allows the child to find his or her way to the nipple. It would seem that from the moment we are born (and indeed prior to birth), we rely on our innate senses of smell, vision and taste to aid in detecting and finding our mother's breast. Alongside our initial breast-tracking senses of smell, vision and taste, our hearing and touch inputs activate a state of comfort and support to get the first of many jobs done. I recommend the research from Klaus and Kennel as an enlightening read for any parent-to-be: www.breastcrawl.org/science.

As any healthy newborn will show us, the moment we come into the world (and indeed prior), our neurology is ready to receive sensory inputs: visual/sight, auditory/hearing, kinaesthetic/touch, olfactory/smell and gustatory/taste for the earliest of tasks. We are also ready from the moment we are born to begin experiencing our external world and collecting sensory information for present and future use.

I invite you to think about that for a moment – all of the experiences we have had from the moment we were born (and in fact prior to birth) are collected and stored in our neurology, like an organic hard drive that is accessed throughout our lives. So is it really a surprise that we often find ourselves behaving in ways that feel as though someone else is at the controls?

An understanding of neuroscience is not necessary to appreciate how, as kids, we were all able to learn a wide range of actions long before verbal instructions were ever an option. Just being present to the behaviours of our earliest care providers was enough to take in what was going on and to model via areas in our brain that have developed specifically for copying those around us.

Mirror, mirror

In the laboratory that is my home kitchen, I created a mini experiment to test some hugely important findings about the human brain's process for learning.

When my son was around five months old, I asked him one morning if I could run my little experiment on him and he smiled in response. I took that as a 'yes' and then placed him in his seat with a mirror in front of him. He is the easiest person to get a smile from, so I smiled at him for two seconds before he broke into another grin. In front of the mirror, with me off to the side and out of his line of sight, he stared curiously at the little person looking back at him. I then poked my head above the mirror and provoked one more smile before moving again out of sight.

The little person in the mirror smiled back at my son, who he smiled back at and continued to smile at for 20 seconds before getting distracted sideways. In this, not very scientific, set-up, my boy was mirroring his own behaviours in the part of his brain that is seemingly designed for this precise purpose.

In the 1990s, an Italian neurophysiology team headed by Dr Giacomo Rizzolatti made a discovery at the University of Parma that would later be heralded by many as the most important neuro-scientific finding of the 20th century. Dr Rizzolatti and his colleagues had implanted electrodes into the brains of a number of macaque monkeys for the purpose of studying their brain activity when the monkeys were engaged in motor actions, or movements, such as holding and lifting objects. During a break from the research process, one of the scientists reached towards an object of some kind and a monitor buzzed to alert him that motor activity was firing in the brain of one of his research monkeys. The macaque's brain was active in the same area as when it made a physical movement of lifting an object with its own hand. Except that, in this instance, the monkey had not moved at all and was simply sitting still watching the human move his hand.

This moment of scientific serendipity was one of many at Parma that opened avenues of research and discovery regarding a particular class of brain cells, now known as 'mirror neurons', that are present in other primates such as humans.

Many years of subsequent studies have provided strong evidence that sets of mirror-neuron systems are responsible for transforming what we see into knowledge of both the intention of another's actions, as well as learning the viewed act for ourselves. No verbal instruction is required, the mere observation of the action is enough. Which gives the phrase 'monkey see, monkey do' a whole new validity.

The renowned neuroscientist, Vilayanur Ramachandran, has gone as far as suggesting that these mirror neurons shaped the beginnings of modern culture and civilisation. Skills such as tool use, fire use and shelter-building, language and the ability to read or interpret another's intentions all happen very quickly and possibly as a result of a sudden emergence of this system that allows us to learn from what we observe.

Instruction manuals or handy tips would not have been of any use to us as kids because language and its meaning arrive much later than our immediate need for basic behaviours. Pre-language, our neurology soaks up a multitude of movement patterns, which we later call 'emotions', 'feelings', 'behaviours' and 'habits' when we are adults.

Walking is the classic example of an entirely copied behaviour. At no point in my son's short walking career have I said to him, 'Hey, dude, put your left foot forward and then find a balance point between your back right foot. Now shift forward and ...'

Just as we can copy an infinite degree of positive behaviours such as upright walking, smiling and lifting a spoon to our mouth, we can also paint onto the canvas of our neurology an equal amount of undesirable traits. Those sudden and unexpected fears, anxieties, anger, violence, jealousy, procrastination and even poor states of health are picked up when we have little choice over their acquisition. Mirror neurons and the connecting parts of our nervous system could be compared to the Switzerland of the brain that seems to remain neutral in decisions of what is good or bad, right or wrong, as they go about integrating what we see into what we do. Regardless of how old we are, both the positive and negative behavioural patterns of our earliest influencers are lingering around in our neurology, just waiting to be activated.

Know nothing

One of the limitations we might face as adults is that of being less curious about the world around us and how it works. For some people, the more they live, the less open they are to life and new experiences. Which is an obvious drawback if we are looking to create change in our lives.

It can be a challenge to approach new learning events without immediately jumping to interpret and evaluate through our existing filters, which exist in the form of our beliefs, values and generalisations of our experiences, from the past up to the present day. Perceptual filters are used by all of us as we go about interpreting our world through what we have learned from our culture and education. It's likely that no two people have ever had an identical experience; because no two people have had identical lives from the moment they were conceived, not even twins. Like you, my own view of the world has been formed by everything I have learned up to this point. Is my view of the world an entirely accurate one? No, but I consider it to be a lot more accurate than some views, which in itself is a filter.

Remaining free from imposing our filters on an experience is easier said than done. The so-called confirmation, or 'my-side', bias is a process that we all engage in from time to time. This is when an individual or group interprets information in such a way that it confirms and fits with their preconceived belief about a subject.

Even experts who have access to research and data can get swept up in imposing their own information filters and biases upon the world. In the sixties, a group of 20,679 physicians apparently gave their approval to a well-known cigarette brand, no doubt because the evidence they sought at the time 'proved' that smoking was good for the throat and lungs, despite the rising incidents of chest infections that were being observed with an increase of tobacco use. How could ill health be linked to smoking if the science from manufacturers was already accepted as fact by such authorities as doctors, though likely doctors who were happily addicted to nicotine? I wonder what our generation's equivalent to cigarettes will turn out to be in the future.

The more expert or informed we are on a subject, the trickier it becomes to remain free of biases. When seeking great teachers, mentors, advisers or coaches it's worth finding the ones who actively go out of their way to find the flaws and weaknesses in their own theories and methods. This 'open-minded' attitude of looking at what we believe, what we do and how we can always improve is one of the most effective first steps towards transforming our lives.

Blank canvases

In Japanese Zen, the term 'beginner's mind' is used to refer to a state of experiencing life through fresh eyes, with curiosity, enthusiasm and without preconceived notions of how or what will come next. Even if the eyes belong to a seasoned expert, the beginner's mind is a reminder that we can always learn, regardless of how well we think we already know what is in front of us. To have a true beginner's mind implies that we drop all of our beliefs, values and assumptions and that we are fully present to what is, rather than what we assume is. This way of applying our attention has become increasingly popular through the application of 'mindfulness', in which millions of people now use phone apps and online platforms for bringing their awareness inwards upon the sensations they experience. Mindfulness can be practised with eyes closed, such as in traditional meditation, or with eyes open, viewing the outside world with total attention and no inner dialogue. Bringing attention to our physical experience is a simple concept that may sound easy, but is a difficult exercise to sustain for more than a few seconds for the majority of us.

You can try it now by setting a stopwatch for 30 seconds and attempting to remain free of thoughts of any kind ...

Tricky, huh?

The benefits of creating a beginner's mind/state, or 'know-nothing' state, is that we can use it as a starting point to bypass what our mirror neurons enabled us to swallow as kids and start to free ourselves from many of the unwanted influences from our history.

Attention!

The first steps in learning how to change and choose how we feel, or precisely, to choose our state is to start with an attention exercise that is similar to mindfulness practice. In my world, the preferred terminology for this is 'self-calibration'. The ability to self-calibrate is an essential ability for creating good health and awareness of our own needs. Some people are naturally very aware of what goes on throughout their body and will act upon the sensations that arise. The kind of experiences I am referring to are the conscious sensations signalling unconscious needs, such as the urge for sleep when tired, to eat when hungry, to walk away when we sense danger, to stop activities that are causing pain, and to regularly respond to the sensations that arise from the non-stop biological processes happening beyond our everyday awareness.

When it comes to optimum health and performance, it is impossible to overstate the importance of training our awareness towards, and responding to, the sensations we experience throughout our system, be that with food and drink, rest and relaxation or using the patterns in this book to change negative, reactive feelings and behaviours.

There's no doubt that some people can go long periods, even whole lifetimes, ignoring the signals and sensations that arise from the unconscious processes that run, and are, our biology. But rarely are those signals ignored without a cost. For example, allowing our blood sugar to drop for long periods has a hugely negative impact upon our metabolism; running on a sleep deficit has been linked to memory loss, impaired learning, stress and degenerative disease; professional athletes regularly end their careers by ignoring early warnings of muscle and joint overuse and who hasn't wished they'd listened to their initial gut warning instincts after an event has taken a turn for the worse?

The more aware we are of our bodily sensations, the more able we become to respond effectively to those needs.

Becoming sensitive to our bodily needs as well as learning to access know-nothing states, can both start with self-calibration of what we are currently experiencing.

The following pattern is effective for both directing attention to our bodily sensations as well as clearing thoughts:

I recommend reading through the following instructions a number of times to get a complete grasp of the steps. You can also visit the Un-train Your Brain website or pass your phone over the QR Code and listen in audio or video format to these instructions.

THE BODY SCAN

The aim of this exercise is to bring your full attention to all areas of your body and become aware of any parts where you hold tension, before then releasing that tension. As you apply the 'tongue-drop' in step 9, you will also experience momentary periods without internal self-talk.

1. Take a moment now, with eyes open, to become completely aware of your body position, be it sitting, standing or lying down.
2. Next, I invite you to hallucinate a beam of horizontal light that is a little more than shoulder-width wide and a few inches in depth. You could compare this to a type of scanner, like a photocopier scan that runs across a page.
3. Once you have a sense of this light, your next step is to move it using your mental control and attention. Hallucinate the light starting at your toes and then rising, scanning upwards and over all your body, to finish at the crown of your head, before then moving back down to your toes again.
4. Keep this image of the scanner in mind, and let it move up and down your body at a pace that allows you to keep your full attention upon it. You can also hallucinate sound as the scanner moves.

5. Slow down the scanner with your attention and mentally instruct or program it to stop at any area of your body where it locates excess muscular tension or tightening.

6. When the scanner locates tension, consciously release that tension by relaxing the affected muscles fully. You may wish to shake or move these muscles around to get them fully loosened.

7. Ensure your scanner hallucination goes slowly over your facial muscles and shoulders.

8. Continue to run the scanner and repeat the muscle relaxing/loosening until your body is without tension.

9. Now drop your tongue forward and down into your lower jaw, just below where the line of your teeth meet the gums. Push your tongue just enough so that it doesn't move at all. If your tongue is still and your body is without tension, you can access a relaxed 'know-nothing' state.

This type of 'know-nothing' experience is unlike how most of us go about our day, because when used effectively it takes us out of our continuous self-chatter. For most people, from the moment we wake we're in our own fixed identities and viewing the world just as we believe it to be. Talking silently to ourselves and reinforcing the who and what we are, with labels and feelings of certainty, which we guard and go out of our way to prove and ensure that we avoid change to our identity at all costs.

All we are is change

Whether we aim to or not, we all change to some small or large degree. Change is at the very essence of life, and yet so often people of all ages will settle for an existence they never wanted. This acceptance is often connected to believing in an identity that declares that this is how or who we are, accompanied by any number of labels that act to confirm and reinforce the fixedness of ourselves.

Are you someone who carries unhelpful labels? Examples could be: 'lazy', 'angry', 'shy', 'helpless', 'cowardly', 'resentful', 'boring', 'chaotic', 'unforgiving', 'obsessed', 'timid', 'demanding', 'depressed', 'conflicted', 'violent', 'victimised', 'repressed', 'paranoid', 'miserable', 'hopeless' or some other.

What are your labels?

As a simple exercise, I invite you to consider what labels you identify with. How might you label your behaviours as if they were actually you?

For example, 'I'm lazy' or 'I'm useless', etc

I am: _____

My next questions are:

1. When and where are you most like this?

2. When and where are you not like this?

It is not uncommon to assume that because we exhibit regular patterns of behaviour at certain times and places, or with certain people, that those behaviours are who we are. But labels can be very dangerous. Not least of all because we may reinforce them with our biases and look for evidence to confirm our faults, rather than look at all the counter-evidence available for how we can also be.

I am guessing it is unlikely your answer to Question 2 was, 'never'.

Have you ever met a person whose behaviour does not change with the situation they are experiencing? For most people, behaviours are influenced by the world around them, which in itself is never static or fixed, so how could a form of behaviour be static or fixed? How could you, or anyone, ever be angry, depressed, hopeless, useless, repressed, shy or some other label, all of the time?

Park it

If you could go back far enough in time before you accepted labels of your own abilities, you would likely see your younger self approaching a wide range of tasks and activities with little or no consideration for failing. At some point in our development we almost certainly approached learning as a game where unintentional mistakes (and in many cases intentional mistakes – the 'I wonder what would happen if ...' approach to experience) were welcomed so that the edge of our current abilities could be known and given new attention before expanding them outwards.

Now, with the passing of time, I invite you to consider the effect on your life if you could choose not to fear or feel embarrassed whenever you failed to get a task correct on the first, second or even tenth attempt?

Please take a minute to answer the following question with as many responses as you can come up with:

'If I had absolutely no fear of failure, I would focus my efforts into achieving ...'

How would not fearing failure of any kind affect your relationship to undertaking these new activities? Would you relish them, like a kid with a new puzzle?

Daily observation of my own kids has confirmed to me how fear of failure is a learned response.

My two-and-a-half-year-old son currently has a fascination with pouring fluids from jugs into cups. Whenever I try to suggest he uses a smaller jug or the big jug with less water, he insists that I stand back and let him get on with it. Luckily our kitchen has floors that can be cleaned easily. His success rate at filling a cup without spilling some, or all, of the jug contents is about 70/30 in favour of spillage. He splashes and covers the floor most of the time. I offer more suggestions and he squarely ignores me. Not once has he turned and said, 'Daddy, I'm not very good at this and won't be trying again.' The same goes for a hundred other daily tasks that he engages in with curiosity and no regard for what failure means.

But now think of the effects on his curiosity, enthusiasm and confidence if I were to interfere with this process, or reprimand him for making yet another mess, tut at him or criticise and label him and his efforts as 'you are clumsy' or 'you're uncoordinated'. It's not difficult to predict how this would affect his relationship with trying new activities and challenges. And at his young age of two and half, if he developed a fear of failure, whose fear would it really be?

Over the years I have been fortunate to spend time with a small number of indigenous cultures and observe remarkable differences between their activities and my own. Rituals, events and behaviours considered normal in the Amazon would be frowned upon, or even illegal, in my home country. What is often a daily practice for some, such as consuming powerful hallucinogens to attract a lover, or eating food that was prepared by women who chewed it and then spat it out, would be bizarre and outlandish for others. It's apparent that we humans are mostly blank canvases until we have the kaleidoscope of outside events imprinted upon our neurology. However, unlike old-fashioned camera films that could only take one exposure, human neurology is more like a digital chip that can be programmed with a potentially infinite degree of new information and content. So whoever and however you may be experiencing the world right now, it is far from fixed. Like it or not, we are all in a constant state of change, some of us changing beneficially and some not, some dramatically, some less so. From the moment we are born, the one guarantee in life is that we all experience change. The question that arises for me to this ever-changing nature of life is a really important one: How do we ensure that the potential for our own change is experienced beneficially?

I have referred to children and our younger selves in this chapter because they are the greatest of life's mirrors and palpably reflect the environment in which they have grown. It would be a really rare person who denied that their earliest influences are often at the source of what they do. As adults, this often makes it easy to assume that the time for personal transformation is long gone and that maybe we missed the boat.

Can you swim? Come on in, the water is lovely ...

Regardless of what our mirror neurons received and what we learned as kids, our neurology has a flexibility that enables us to make new changes. No matter what holds you back, you can shake off the labels, step away from your past reactions and start to achieve your full potential.

CHAPTER 2

FREEDOM FROM LIVING (ONLY) IN YOUR HEAD

There is no mind/body split, only one whole person – a living, conscious state. We each experience and create our own version of reality through what our senses receive from our whole self. Accepting our own version of that reality to be 'true' is a potentially foolish position to take for its limiting effect upon our lives. Having the freedom to shift our own perception is a highly useful part of the solution.

> *'To keep the body in good health is a duty ... otherwise we shall not be able to keep our mind strong and clear.'*
>
> Buddha (allegedly)

I suspect that few of us would congratulate ourselves for having won the evolutionary lottery, even though our ancestors went through a fair amount of hassle for each of us to become one of seven billion champions of the big race we call 'life'. Our earliest relatives seemingly slogged it out over millions of years from single-celled organisms that gradually strengthened and wriggled out of the primordial gloop to an eventual slithering over rocks, then growing of limbs, ultimately, to use those limbs for hitting dinner over the head, then hitting each other over the head (not much has changed there) and then eventually to spending quite a lot of time tapping on a keyboard and staring at little screens with moving pictures and text.

During this long process of trial and error, we have come into possession of possibly the finest, most evolved, most powerful processing unit in the currently known universe: a human nervous system that is run by its main (we assume for now) operating hub – the brain. Having this neurology means that we are capable of contemplating multiple universes, interstellar space, eternity, quantum physics, the nature of reality, the nature of the brain's own brain, questions about the source of life, God, gods, philosophy, mathematics, paradoxes and an endless degree of complexities, known and currently unknown, not to mention lashings of self-delusion.

Your neurology is presently enabling you to experience these words in a form that communicates their meaning (in part at least). It consists of a vast number of those nerve cells known as 'neurons'. It is generally accepted that we have around 100 billion neurons, which is about the same number as trees in the Amazon rainforest, give or take a few mass-deforestation areas.

Each neuron is connected to around 10,000 others, which makes the total number of connections in our brain the same as the number of leaves in the rainforest – a whopping 1,000 trillion, a seemingly immeasurable amount. Some 100,000 chemical reactions happen in our three pounds of fleshy protein and fat every second, along with a corresponding effect in our wider central and peripheral nervous system.

Just recently a collection of these organised neurons and synapses was able to achieve the act of landing a robot probe on a comet that is a half a billion kilometres away from earth. Such events, personally, leave me astonished and guessing at the huge potential of brain power that is yet to be put into use by our species. Similarly, on the very same day, back here on our little blue planet, varying acts of violence were being committed by young men who support opposing football teams; while in yet another country, a number of young women were being punished by an extreme religious group, in the hope that such tactics might impart some form of virtue on the other females of the species who dared to step out of line. Such events also leave me astonished, at the extreme lack of brain power employed, and which to me at least signals a reverse of progress.

There is no doubt that the brain is a complex and seemingly contradictory lump of tofu-like mass inhabiting our craniums, and which, at times, can leave even the smartest of owners wondering how best to operate it.

Oh René!

The majority of interest and research on human consciousness and behaviour focuses mostly upon the brain. But I think it's crucial to broaden our view beyond just our heads and include the whole network that runs throughout us. This means including our entire neurology of the central nervous system (CNS), which consists of the brain and spinal cord as well as the peripheral nervous system (PNS), which the CNS is connected to and which mostly consists of nerves extending throughout our body. Our nervous system regulates our involuntary or 'unconscious' functions, such as heart rate, breathing, digestion and a range of functions that happen in and under our skin and of which we are not usually aware. This unconscious activity includes how our states and awareness of 'mind' connect as one operating unit of activity.

Knowing that our brain is connected to every other part of our body really matters, because to maximise the utility of our neurology requires more than just working on mental processes.

It was René Descartes (1596–1650), French mathematician, philosopher and physiologist who receives a major part of the blame for presenting the theory that our mind and body are split (given the catchy term Cartesian Dualism), though the idea dates as far back as Ancient Greece.

There is no doubt that Descartes' idea seems to fit with much of our conscious experience of life, in that we notice a distinction between thoughts seeming to be non-physical and in the head area, whereas sensations of the body are easier to note in physical locations. But the reality is that our entire body is divided only by a categorisation of parts, which has largely been assigned artificially by physiologists and medical doctors to assist with descriptions and attempts at understanding how we work. Just like the lines on a map that create artificial borders between countries, when the landmass of say 'Europe', is clearly just one big piece of earth that has been divided by the hand of humans, into many smaller countries. In the body, we have named and divided each organ and subset of our body into its functioning parts. This part is attached to that part and so on. At times, this serves a useful purpose as we study the individual functions of a body part or organ and how best to treat any related illness or reduction in function.

But take too many bits off the whole and it is likely to cease functioning well or even at all. I am not saying there is no justification for applying distinct names to various portions of our body – certainly more justification than for a bunch of old fat white guys in Berlin drawing lines on maps in 1884/85. It is just very important to regard ourselves as a whole that exists as a complete living state of matter, energy and intelligence, rather than individual bits and pieces.

The problems that arise from accepting a mind–body split made of many little parts is that we are likely to distinguish our thoughts as being unrelated to our physical experiences and vice-versa. With that acceptance comes the probable priority to one over the other – intellect becomes more important than our ability to climb stairs, or running long distances becomes more important than increasing our ability to think creatively and so on. More crucial still are the effects that negative thoughts can have on our health and states. Just thinking about a scary/exciting/provocative subject will release adrenaline and other fight-or-flight hormones.

We know from a large number of studies that positive people are healthier and that they live for longer. A 30-year study of 447 people conducted by the Mayo Clinic, a world leading medical organisation, found that optimists had around a 50 per cent lower risk of early death than pessimists. A Dutch study showed a 77 per cent lower risk of heart disease in optimists compared to pessimists.

In 1979, a study of 7,000 adults in California revealed that participants who reported fewer social ties at the start of the survey had double the likelihood of death over the nine-year follow-up period. This effect was unrelated to habits such as smoking, drinking and exercise. Social connections included marriage, time with friends and relatives as well as organisational and church memberships.

Despite a lot of medical books telling us otherwise, it actually does not require a great deal of empirical or scientific evidence to realise that there is no mind–body split at all.

After all, when did you last see a person who was given bad news not experience an obvious shift in his or her physiology to match the felt emotion? Can you really imagine a thought without any set of impulses, contractions or releases of the musculature or shifts in the biochemistry? When you last felt ill from a virus or bacteria, did you find that your thoughts were clear and focused on work tasks? My guess is you probably thought of nothing other than how you could hang your head in a bucket or get what you needed to feel well again.

If we closely observe the eyes, facial muscles, breathing, movements and tension in other people we notice a corresponding physical response for the thoughts that are taking place in 'the mind'. You can experiment right now by paying very close attention to your current state.

How would you describe how you feel?

Now make a really big smile and continue to hold this smile for 30 seconds ...

Did you notice a shift in the way you felt? There is evidence that pulling a smiling face has the effect of creating 'happy' feelings, rather than smiling being a consequence of happy feelings. Holding a smile has also been shown to bias some people into recalling more positive memories when asked to think of any past events.

All of our muscles play an enormous role in how we feel. A close friend recently told me of her mother's dramatic lift in mood after receiving Botox injections to her forehead. The mother in question was a real frowner and the sudden freeze of her forehead had the effect of freezing her usual judgemental personality. My friend's mother is far from unique as studies have shown that Botox can interfere with an individual's emotions due to a lack of feedback from the face to the nervous system.

The mind–body belief is important to overcome when we aim to make positive changes in our lives, because we interface with the world as a whole person. When we are physically well, our states, thoughts and actions follow in order. In fact, we are our states, so our thoughts and actions are dependent upon how we exist in synergy, not parts.

What this means for us on a practical level is that by changing our physiology, we get to change our states and thoughts and vice-versa. As an example, could you imagine a well-trained athlete feeling depressed as they engage with their sport, or a singer performing at their best while hunched over?

Try it now. Hunch yourself up tight for a full minute and experience what it does to your state and thoughts.

Next, expand your arms and body skyward in a gentle, wide-open stretch.

Do you notice a difference in more than just your muscles?

A couple of years back, I decided to stand up while performing any work on my computer. I arranged a small shelving unit on top of my desk so that my laptop was at chest height. It is hard to quantify my creativity, but my productivity increased greatly. I have also worked with a couple of writers who were experiencing creative 'blocks'. In such situations I usually recommend gym membership, or access of some kind to a treadmill, so that the writer can walk very slowly on the treadmill with their laptop on a stand in front of them. This has a reliable effect of magically lifting away creative stalling because creativity arises as a consequence of the state we are in, and our state can be influenced positively by moving upright rather than statically hunching over. I invite you to put this knowledge to the test right now using the simplest of exercises.

PATTERN/EXERCISE:

Making states

In this exercise I invite you to spend a minute walking around as if you are experiencing three different unwanted states. These should be mildly unpleasant states and not anything too serious for you. You might want to choose boredom, annoyance, frustration, disappointment, or some other state of similar effect.

To intentionally experience these states, recall a time and place when you experienced them and 'associate' into the experience by seeing and hearing the memory through your own eyes and ears. As you do, consider:

- What your posture looks like from an observer's view of you
- How your facial expressions display those states
- Whether your breathing has changed
- How these states play out in the way you move your limbs

Before moving on to the next step, give your body a thorough shake to shift any unwanted sensations that might be in your system.

Now repeat the same walk while experiencing three desirable states, such as confidence, joy, curiosity, – or whatever you choose.

As you do so, consider:

- What your posture looks like from an observer's view of you
- How your facial expressions display those states
- Whether your breathing has changed
- How these states play out in the way you move your limbs

The more clearly you recall and experience these states through your posture, facial expressions and actions, the more you will notice their effect upon the way you feel.

This is a useful exercise for experiencing how our feelings are influenced by our physiology.

How do we know?

Our personal experiences are made up of the information we take in from our senses, individually and collectively. Every idea, memory, value, belief, preference and dream is available to us because of the rich catalogue of sensory information we each experience and store in our nervous system, making us uniquely, but temporarily, who we are. In essence, the building blocks of each of us are those units of sensory information received by our neurology since it began developing when we were in the womb.

We are seemingly made up of what comes through our senses.

Hallucinate for a brief moment that you have a box with five switches in front of you. They are labelled: 'sight', 'hearing', 'feeling', 'smell', 'taste'. The switches are on–off switches as labelled for each sense. A researcher switches off your 'sight' switch. Now consider your world: 'It's rather dark in here!' Now she switches off 'hearing'. Did you just step into a vacuum? All at once, the experimenter switches off the remaining senses that remove your feelings, taste and smell, on top of the previous loss of sight and sound.

Who are you and how do you know who you are at this point?

This is a tricky question to attempt to answer as you have no point of reference to be able to do so, even though consciousness is still present, it would have no relationship to the inside or outside world. So how would you know that you were even knowing?

Each of us captures information from and about the world around us and then creates our own version of an inner model or 'map' of what is actually 'out there'. We all have these little maps that are learned guides on how to respond to the world.

Another way of looking at it is that we each build a personalised reality, specific to our own needs. This inner construction has been described quite effectively as 'a reality tunnel' by the late LSD guru, Timothy Leary. The tunnel metaphor is a valuable one because it highlights the narrow limitations of our own views of the world, compared to what really exists in the vastness of actual reality.

Human-reality tunnels are culturally distinct, encased by our learned values, experiences and beliefs and we each reinforce them by the strength and narrowness of the vocabulary that accompanies our particular form of world-view, along with the actions and ideas that spring forth from it.

Imagine a suicide bomber who whips himself into a religious fever with talk of 'one true God, the infallibility of his dogma and religion', 'Jihad', 'infidels' and 'eternity in paradise' for his actions. It is unlikely that such a person talks about his or her beliefs with any uncertainty: 'Well, I'm happy to consider that there is no verifiable evidence for or against (a) God(s), and I suspect, or rather, hope that there might be a possibility of living in a potential paradise with all those alleged virgins ... maybe ...' Followed by, 'Uh, can someone please get this ticking clock off me – NOW!' Remaining open to doubt and being wrong about our personal positions is not always easy, but to avoid doing so comes with a cost: tick, tock ...

Our desire to know certain specifics about 'true reality' is important to some of us, but even if you are a scientist, the most you can do is to pin little flags in your maps that represent how you have organised the external, internally. It is no absolute reality, but we get to experience our version of it more comfortably this way.

You, like me, have likely met lots of people who are very firm in their views. I know that I have been personally guilty, many a time, of having an inflexible position on certain points that I am passionate about. There is rarely much objectivity in these views, unless I'm arguing about the lack of objectivity in views! If you're someone who is curious and courageous enough to want to break out of your own reality tunnel, you can do so effectively by using patterns that increase perception and widen our capture of information.

Shifting perception

There are three useful positions of perception that we can take in any event or context. When used together, these perceptual positions broaden our world-view and provide a more complete and useful way of gathering information. This can lead to a clearer appreciation of other people's and our own needs and behaviours.

We will use and come back to these positions throughout this book.

The perceptual positions are as shown in the following diagram:

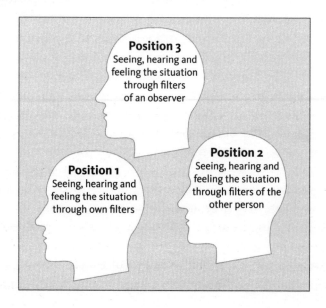

First Position: Seeing, hearing and feeling the situation through our own filters.

Second Position: Seeing, hearing and feeling the situation through the filters of the other person.

Third Position: Seeing, hearing and feeling the situation through the filters of an observer.

First Position

If you have ever debated with someone who was steadfast in their ideas, you will know that he or she had very little appreciation of your own perception of the subject. When we hold tight to our own ideas, beliefs and values and experience the world only through our own senses, we are in First Position. In this position, there is very little objectivity or appreciation for other perceptual positions. High-performance sportsmen, musicians, military personnel and anyone who strongly experiences their bodily sensations in the moment are mostly in First Position.

It is valuable to have a healthy personal identity and awareness of our own needs. However, a drawback of living entirely in First Position is to disregard the feelings, needs and positions of everyone else.

Second Position

Most of us naturally access a Second Position (possibly due to the previously mentioned mirror neurons or some similar 'empathy' area of the brain) and we are able to observe and appreciate the feelings of others to varying degrees.

Effective therapists, coaches, negotiators and parents use the ability to step into Second Position and get a sense of how the other person's map of their world has been created.

If you think back to the previous chapter (Chapter 1, Freedom from what?), you will realise that children tend to use the Second Position when they copy and model behaviours, so it is as natural a position to take as is our own First Position.

Some people live too much in Second Position and are unable to make decisions for themselves, become too dependent upon, or worry about, the opinions of other people. I once attended a large, very formal, wedding where the only two men wearing regular suits (as opposed to tailed morning suits) were me and a younger, immaculately groomed, chap. During the reception he approached me and asked how I felt about not wearing the appropriate formal wear. I replied that I had relied upon my wife to read the invitation and was therefore at fault for not checking the dress code myself. But so what, I said, it is an easy mistake to make and no one cares about how I look, I am not the groom! His response was that he felt everyone was critical of us and that it was deeply disrespectful to the wedding couple. He could not take the staring any more and had decided to go home and change. By the time he had arrived back again most of the men had their jackets off, sleeves rolled up and a glass of bubbly in their hand!

The skill of accessing a Second Position comes with many benefits, such as creating agreements, empathy and bridging understanding in negotiation, which is an essential element to any domestic or professional relationship.

Third Position

If you have ever been to the theatre you will know how easy it is to identify with the actors playing their various roles upon the stage. However rarely do you identify so much so that when an actor falls to the ground playing at being shot or ill, you then rush forward to administer treatment. You can, in this instance, observe without being emotionally compelled to act.

You also know, from observing your own friends and family members, just how easy it is to see where they are making poor choices in their lives. You may even wish that they could see what you can see them doing. When we access a Third Position perspective, it can provide us with an effective way to observe our own behaviours and then offer constructive suggestions on how to behave differently.

I often wonder how people get by without the use of a Third Position. I suspect that after you have used it on a couple of occasions, you will wonder as well.

Third Position creates different states than does First or Second Position. The Third Position is more objective and neutral, free of any emotional charge.

As with overuse of any of the positions, if we stay in Third Position too much we can fail to experience the emotions and states associated with First. As an example, one client has a father who is so emotionally neutral, logical and removed that she has never once felt that he appreciates or understands her. She has never heard him shout, lose his temper or become emotional with her and he is always fair and does the 'right thing'. In return, the client has become entirely detached from her father and though she knows he has all her best interests in mind, she and he share almost zero emotional connection.

Third is the position for being your own coach and providing feedback on your own performance. This use of our perception is enlightening and, when practised regularly, can have the profound effect of single-handedly shifting many of our undesirable behaviours. This one pattern alone has the potential to un-train our brains.

To use our perceptual positions requires a shift in how we already think and observe. We are simply accessing natural abilities rather than creating something new.

I offer an example of how someone might begin using these positions:

Sally sits in a chair, slouching and watching TV. She wants some motivation to work on a project. To use her Third Position, she stands up, steps away from her chair and looks back to hallucinate Sally (herself) slouching and watching TV where she was a second ago.

Now standing in Third Position she straightens her spine and relaxes her body. She then offers the following feedback to the memory of herself in the chair: 'Sally, you are slouching and this is bad for your back. You are also wasting time and procrastinating in front of a bad TV show. Get up and get on with the work you know you have to finish before the end of the week. Turn the TV off and get some fresh air into this room. Think about how good you will feel when you have completed your work on time. Can you feel that? Good, now get on with it and take the first, smallest step.'

Sally now sits back in the (slouch) position she originally filled and receives the advice from her Third Position, to be utilised immediately.

Being able to view events from multiple perceptual positions has a wide range of uses. In my coaching work, I access Second Position to get an appreciation of my client's needs. If I ever get stuck when working with a client or come up against blocks in my other projects, I step out to Third Position and provide feedback and instructions on how to move forward.

You can also utilise these perceptual positions for planning, building empathy, taking a breather from stressful contexts, working out why you get certain results and outcomes and, best of all, integrating all of these uses, and more, to become your own coach and adviser.

My Third Position has literally saved my hide on more occasions than I can recall and after some regular use of these patterns, you will likely find that you automatically begin accessing different perceptual positions without any physical need to move into a new location. With practice we can create a pattern of effortlessly adjusting our perception in an automatic way, with little conscious effort.

PATTERN: INSTALLING PERCEPTUAL POSITIONS

Steps for First Position

1. To experience First Position, take a moment to run the scanner from Chapter 1 (see page 24), up and down your body, noticing all of the sensations occurring.

2. Ask yourself a general, life question: what is most important to you right now, above all else? Now notice what feelings you experience while thinking about the answer.
3. Think of something you really believe (meaning you do not have actual evidence for it) and now hallucinate someone opposite you telling you that your belief is unfounded and a load of baloney.
4. Notice, without labelling them, the sensations that arise from the previous three suggestions.

Steps for Second Position

To experience Second Position requires that you first identify the person you wish to take a Second Position on. This could be someone, such as a potential employer or troubled friend, you are currently having a dispute with, or have a reason for wanting a fuller appreciation of what he or she is experiencing. You can access Second Position with a person who is physically present or based on your memory and knowledge of that person.

I will assume you are in the presence of the person you wish to have a Second Position on.

1. A beginner's mind/know-nothing state is the first step and can be achieved through reducing your internal chatter, by gently pushing and dropping your tongue forward in your lower jaw. Place your attention on keeping your tongue pushed forward enough so that it does not move. This has the effect of limiting internal thoughts and self-talk with yourself and creates something of an empty mind.
2. Now breathe in rhythm with the person you are observing and begin to mirror their movements and gestures with micro-muscle movements. This pattern of matching the other person's physiology with micro-muscle mirroring means that if they move their arm, you move just enough as

if you were going to make the same gesture, but so slight that it is *unobservable* to the other person. You will feel the movement as if you had made the same gesture, but the other person won't see it because it is a micro-movement.

3. Repeat this micro-muscle mirroring with all of the other person's body movements, including their head tilts and facial expressions. Regardless of how the other person is moving, you mirror their gestures with the smallest of matching movements.

4. Next, hallucinate that you can float into their body and see through their eyes, hear with their ears and feel what they feel. Become this person for long enough that you get to experience the world as they do.

I am often surprised at the ideas and intuition that arise when I use Second Position in this way. As a coach, it gives me a deep insight into how my clients live their problems, so that when I return to my own First Position, I can bring back useful information for our work together. In any situation where you want a better appreciation of what the other person is experiencing, use Second Position in this way.

As a light warning, it is really important that after you experience a Second Position on someone, before moving on you fully re-associate to your First Position and remind yourself of what it is to live through your own senses. Forgetting to do so can have some interesting consequences, including making decisions you wouldn't usually make.

Steps for Third Position

1. It is best to experience Third Position immediately after an activity, let's say reading these instructions in this book. To access Third Position, physically move to a new position a few feet away, where you can now observe the empty space

that you previously occupied seconds ago, performing the activity – in this case reading these instructions.

2. Move into a new physical location and look back at where you were previously as in step 1. Now adjust your physiology/posture to become more upright, with straightened spine, relaxed shoulders and deep, slow breath.

3. Using your memory, look back and see yourself undertaking the activity of reading these instructions, in the space you previously filled. You are now in Third Position, and with a little practice you can view your previous performance and offer objective feedback on how you were doing. You can now offer your First Position suggestions of specific changes in the behaviours you see.

4. Once you have finished giving feedback from Third Position, step back into the space where you started, First Position, and receive the feedback as if you are hearing your Third Position adviser or coach give the advice just offered.

You: a living research laboratory

It can be strikingly obvious to us when other people are in need of making changes in their lives. You may have observed your own colleagues, friends and family play out patterns of behaviour that only a fool would be blind to, and this is a common consequence of being too fixed in any of the three possible perceptual positions. Flexibility in the views we take can enable us to get useful information about others and ourselves and also ensure that we do not live too ignorantly in our own version of reality.

When we take time to distance ourselves from our own maps or reality tunnels and take in more of the information on offer from life, we get a broader, more reliable, version of what reality could be, including all of the untapped potential in each of us that is waiting to be set free.

I would like to propose that from here on you become like a scientific researcher or an explorer arriving in strange lands. Your mission is to begin observing from Third and Second Positions how you do what you do to create the life you currently inhabit.

As Socrates stated, 'the unexamined life is not worth living'. So let's examine some more ...

CHAPTER 3

FREEDOM FROM EXCUSES

Though we may not always be able to make the choices we most desire, we always have the freedom to choose how we respond to a situation. This places responsibility for our lives firmly in our own hands.

> *'You can't blame gravity for falling in love.'*
>
> Albert Einstein

In my twenties I climbed many hundreds of rock climbs all over the world. On one particular climbing trip to France, I was feeling strong and fit as I confidently started upwards on a climb I had easily ascended a year before. However on this particular day, within a few short moves, I had placed my hands in the wrong order, which meant that I used up double the required energy to reach the difficult point higher in the climb. At the crucial move my state-of-the-art climbing shoes slid on some of the tiny holds that had become highly polished from overuse. With lactic acid filling my forearms and stamina reserves running low, I rushed into the difficult section of the climb. I scrambled my feet, made hesitant, jerky movements and lunged for a tiny finger pocket. I missed, cartwheeled outwards and took a small, safe fall onto my rope.

I have been a climber for over 20 years and I estimate that I have taken many hundreds, if not a thousand falls over that time. This particular fall was nothing special and far from spectacular. So, to the casual observer, it would have made little sense to witness what I did next. In a screaming, shouting rage of disgust and anger, I directed my attention first at the rock – slapping it for its sins, followed by tearing off my new climbing shoes, screaming about the awful quality of the rubber, along with another jab and scream about the terrible quality of the polished, shitty French rock. My attention then turned to the appalling quality of my climbing partner's belaying and lack of encouragement, finished with a spraying of profanities about how terrible France and everything French was. My reaction was all-consuming and I lost myself in it for a good half minute or so before throwing my shoes as hard as I could into the surrounding woodland. It later took me over an hour to find that left shoe.

You could say I was pretty passionate about the sport back then, which was certainly my excuse for the extreme over-reaction. But did I react because the climb was important to me? Or was my reaction because the rock had become more slippery due to its popularity and more climbers ascending it? Maybe it was because my climbing partner's rope skills and lack of encouragement did contribute to my fall? At the time, I used the word 'because' a lot. I failed and fell because ...

But when it comes to our human responses to a stimulus, the word 'because' really has no valid place in our vocabulary. Why? Well, because ...

When we use the word 'because' as a justification for our actions, we engage the idea of cause/effect, which though valid in many biological processes, physics and the interactions of non-conscious things, has no real validity in the choices that people make.

The late, great anthropologist, Gregory Bateson, provided an elegant metaphor to upset or liberate any regular maker of cause/effect-style excuses. Think for a moment that you are standing in a field with a ball in front of you. An engineer is present who calibrates all the relevant measurements of the ball – surface area, weight, size, etc. You kick the ball and, again, the engineer is able to measure the speed, angle and direction of your kick, along with external factors such as wind speed. Using an equation that is hundreds of years old, the engineer can predict where the ball will land, with inch-precision.

Even if you repeatedly change to different balls, as long as the accurate measurements are in place, the engineer can predict the landing position of each ball. Now change the ball for an entirely different object. Similarly, you have all of the weights, size and surface area of the new object. In fact, you even know what it ate for breakfast … The new object is a live cat. You (only conceptually) kick the cat under the same previous measurement conditions. The question is, can the engineer predict where the cat will land?

Maybe on a first kick, there is the slightest chance that the cat's flight can be predicted to some vague direction or distance, but accuracy is simply out of the question. On both the first, and especially the second, kick, the possibility exists for the cat to dig its claws into your ankle, groin, or throat, to run sideways, jump into the air … in fact, there is an unlimited number of responses available to the cat.

Why?

Like you, me and all living creatures, the cat has *choice* and is able to choose a response to a stimulus.

Under pressure

One of the most dramatic examples of choice response that I ever heard of was by a colleague who had a life-changing epiphany under one of the most stressful situations imaginable.

Jim: 'After the fifth time, I just got to a point that I thought, go ahead, blow a big fucking hole in my head, I'm not giving you the satisfaction of me shitting my pants any more.'

Jim had once been a full member of the US Navy SEALs. After years of active service, he left and undertook private security work, protecting cargo shipments along the African coast. He, along with a dozen other non-military-trained workers, were taken hostage (by pirates) and held for six weeks until the insurance company paid the required ransom. In that time, Jim had been identified as the military-trained member of the hostage group and was tortured on a daily basis; or at least his captors assumed they were torturing him.

On the second morning of captivity, Jim was told that he would be executed, to show the insurance company just how serious the pirates' threats were if it was not paid on time. Jim was hooded, pulled from his cell and dragged into a courtyard. When the hood was removed, one of his captors held a rusty Kalashnikov to his head. They informed him of his imminent death, and Jim, through gritted teeth, noted that, not for the first time in his life, he was scared to the point of being completely overwhelmed. In clichéd fashion, he saw images of his life rush through his field of vision and then the last thing he heard was the click of the rifle …

Is it true that we always have choice, no matter what the situation?

That's a question I asked and challenged myself to answer a hundred or more times until I truly appreciated and grasped the concept.

Every time that we react in a reflexive, habitual way, and then hear ourselves justify our actions, we are relying upon a belief that takes away our ownership of how we felt (our states) and the decisions we made in those states. I wish I had a ten-dollar bill for every time I caught myself in a finger-pointing position when something was not working, and then had the good sense to ask: 'Am I a cat or a ball?'

The potential outcomes of that answer are vastly different. One outcome takes full responsibility for the choices they make, the other outcome hands responsibility over to the weather, genetics, God, hidden sugars, politics, school, the universe or … name your cause.

You will likely recognise your own use of cause/effect being played out in relationships when you falsely accept and then express a belief that another person, group, organisation or event can dictate and control the way you feel and act. If you happen to live in a blame culture, it often makes it all too easy to say, 'it's not my fault'.

Maybe you tell your partner that they made you lose your temper and so consequently you kicked the dog (I am giving cats a break for now).

The question is how exactly your partner got into your neurology to do this? Or does your partner have a digital control pad that directs you, robot-like, to feel and behave in ways that are against your own choosing? Can your partner – or indeed anyone – ever make you do or feel what you did not want to do, even with a gun to your head?

Cause/effect can play out in less provocative contexts as well. As an example, one person might say that she loved a hotel *because* of its antique décor and traditional feel, while another expresses her dislike *because* of the old-fashioned furniture and outdated themes. It is the same hotel, but two entirely different ways of organising the information about it. Nothing of the actual hotel experience is objective to the guests experiencing it. The conclusion that the guests love or dislike the hotel because of its furniture cannot be sustained. They love or dislike the hotel due to their unique filters that have been created by a billion small influences in their neurology since they were born, many of which remain unconscious to them.

The question is, which of those billion experiences are responsible for the guests' opinions?

Ask yourself right now why you prefer a certain food over another?

You like that food because ...

But are you sure, of all the influences in your life that lead to this decision of preference, that your stated reason is THE only reason?

Very few people are free from cause/effect in their language patterns, and you yourself may have uttered or heard one or more of the following phrases that are commonly used – I suspect without the appropriate challenges that accompany the questions on the next page.

Statement: You make me angry.
Question: How does my behaviour control your response?

Statement: He made me crash.
Question: At what point was he in charge of your vehicle?

Statement: Look what you made me do.
Question: How specifically did I move your limbs to do that?

Statement: You made him look like an idiot.
Question: Which of my actions changed his appearance?

Statement: Can you make him win?
Question: Can you make the other competitors lose?

Statement: He makes her happy.
Question: How does he get into her nervous system and mimic those feel-good hormones and neurotransmitters?

When it comes to your own responses, actions and behaviours, where and when do you use or accept expressions such as:

- 'It's because of'
- 'You made me'
- 'It's their fault'
- 'I can't do that, so I did this'
- 'She/he makes me'
- 'Due to'
- 'He/she told me to'
- 'As a consequence of'
- 'I did it because someone did it to me'
- 'Owing to'
- 'Thanks to'

I invite you to consider what the outcomes, results and consequences are that you experience when you fail to challenge these verbal cause/effect patterns?

Do they support and enable you to create positive change in your life? (You can write in the space below or use your own notebook or journal.)

What are the consequences/outcomes of accepting cause/ effect in:

My relationships

My career

My health

My finances

My personal development

What are the possibilities/consequences/outcomes when you do not accept cause/effect in:

My relationships

My career

My health

My finances

My personal development

One of my clients, Rich, likes to drink so much that he would be called an alcoholic in most circles. He had an abusive father and was arrested for minor crimes as a teenager. He was out of work for a number of years in his early twenties and has a past he is not proud of. Now, in his thirties, he blames his present drinking pattern on these past events.

Here are small parts of our first conversation:

Rich: 'I drink because of my past.'

Mike: 'How does your past create so much thirst?'

Rich: 'Drink removes the pain.'

Mike: 'Does this drink have a surgeon licence?'

Rich: 'You don't understand. Alcohol separates me from all my anger and hatred.'

Mike: 'Where does it put those states while you're drunk? Does it have a special location?'

Rich: 'What else can I do?'

Mike: 'Learn to choose your states when you recall those past events, so that you can experience them without feeling the need to escape, along with many other more useful activities.'

Clients regularly object to my push for personal responsibility to this degree. One lady angrily told me, 'I've been in pain for months because someone else knocked me off my bicycle.'

I asked her, 'Are you in pain because you haven't taken the physiotherapy treatment seriously and skipped the daily routines you were given?' (I knew this to be the case.)

'Or are you in pain because you're overweight from over-eating and your body has too much pressure weighing down on your injuries?'

'Are you in pain because you haven't taken the supplements that have been proven to reduce inflammation?'

'Is your pain because you were riding your bicycle badly?'

'Is your pain because you rode a bicycle at all?'

My intention is not to belittle or take away from the experience this lady was having, but to give her back her choice over the pain and prevent her from allowing similar passive, victim patterns of thought and actions to play out in her life in the future.

When do you allocate exterior causes for your own choices and behaviours? (Either write in the spaces provided here or use your personal notebook or journal.)

Example:

I experience ___ *dread* _____ because of ___ *the economy* _____

I experience _____ because of _____

I experience _____ because of _____

I experience _____ because of _____

I experience _____ because of _____

A warrior way

My special forces' colleague, Jim, used the term 'crapping myself', even though he never physically carried out this action. He was too well trained to lose bowel control. However, the fear that accompanies the belief that your last moments will be spent kneeling in an African pirate hideout is more than enough to blur the lines between conscious and unconscious waking states.

For five consecutive days, the pirates tormented Jim by confirming that this really was the day of his death. On day six, they still stated their intentions to kill him and went through the charade of doing so, though Jim had no idea if it was a charade until the end. What was noticeable to anyone with the ability to really see was that on this sixth day, Jim walked taller, did not resist the usual drag from his cell, breathed slowly and steadily and failed to make any unconscious murmurs or groans.

The previous night, he had made a decision. If he was going to be executed or once again go through the daily mental torture of believing that he was, he would do it without fear or cowardice. His decision was based upon two elements he could identify:

1. He hated his captors' cruelty and did not want to give these men the satisfaction of seeing his fear.
2. The realisation and acceptance that he, alone, was choosing to experience fear in this situation, when, in fact, he could find a multitude of other preferable feelings to take the place of fear.

Jim experienced a crystal-clear lucidity that even though he had no choice over the gun being loaded or not, he still had complete choice over how he faced the trigger being pulled.

> **Jim:** 'I spent the entire night facing my own ideas of death. I remembered some of my favourite stories about Samurai warriors facing their final moments with calm and serenity. So I chose to face up to my daily dance with death as an old-school warrior would. That was the moment I stopped being afraid.'

By the end of his capture period, Jim had received over 30 false executions and numerous beatings. He tells me that the first five executions were horrific, while the rest taught him who he really was.

Individuals like Jim are trained over years to a degree of conditioning and control that few of us will ever know. However, Jim's training was still not enough to prevent the choices he made leading up to his capture. Ultimately, his situation focused him on the one very important process he still had complete choice over: the way he chose to feel.

If we track back, at some point Jim also had a choice over being on the Somali coast in the first place. The very situation he chose to step into was one in which dire consequences can be experienced if plans go wrong. In the same way, the child who gets bullied may not feel he has choice over his situation (assuming he is too young to have yet mastered his feelings), but as long as he continues to place himself within the bully's reach, this remains mostly true. But does the child (or the special forces' veteran) have any other choices in the initial stages of the sequence of events? Possibly so, and by ensuring that this option is apparent, it restores some level of choice to the 'victim' so that he or she can take a different route the next time they face such possibilities.

Jim went back to school after his ordeal and now teaches hostage-negotiation training in Los Angeles. He never went back to such hostile countries and is not likely to do so in the future.

Reason to smile

I am a member of a small emergency-response team that delivers medical and post-traumatic stress relief to disaster-affected countries. In 2010, shortly after the earthquake that killed an estimated 260,000 people, I flew to Haiti for the first of many ongoing visits.

Like too many of my earliest clients in Haiti, I fail to remember the lady's name. However, I have a distinct memory of her face and especially how immaculately well dressed she was, despite living in an IDP (internally displaced people) camp along with 50,000 other homeless people, surrounded by mud and protected only by blue tarpaulin sheets. Similar to many other Haitian women I had met, she had a proud, almost noble, countenance. When I asked how I could help, she made an admission to me in a guilty fashion, as if the sharing was a great shame or wrong she was a part of. Her English was clear, even as she caught her breath while speaking to me:

Lady: 'I am having desperate thoughts and feelings, and I do not know how I can go on.'

As she forced the words from her lips, her whole body was racked in sobs. We spoke of what had happened in the previous two months since the earthquake. Her story was similar to many I had heard since being in the country. She was an extremely well-educated woman who had worked full-time at a school for primary-age kids of between seven and eleven years. If there had been a minuscule amount of good fortune to be found in the quake, it was that it happened minutes before 5pm, which meant that most kids had left the school and were either at home or playing outside. Her school had been completely destroyed and many of her fellow teachers had died when it collapsed. A number of her students had also died in their homes, as had her own relatives. Her home was now rubble; hence she was living in a tent.

Long before assisting in Haiti, I had learned that I would be incapable of working effectively if my empathy wasn't dissociated from other people's suffering. In such situations it is too easy to get lost in people's stories, unless you know how to choose to remain free of a full Second Position. In my first week of working with over 100 homeless and, at times, desperate individuals, I had heard more heart-breaking accounts of events than in all my previous years combined. Choosing to feel sorry for this lady was neither going to help her nor me in the long run, so during her tearful description of life in the camp, I unexpectedly threw a full plastic cup of water over her.

My translator let out a loud breath as I just stared at the lady with a look of contempt. Not contempt for her ordeal, just total contempt for her current state of feeling desperate.

> **Lady:** (with a shocked look on her face) 'I do not understand why you did this?'
>
> **Mike:** 'I wanted to stop you from doing any more self-pity. I see the spark of the smart, capable and resourceful woman in front of me who has no chance of changing her situation as long as she is crying about it.'
>
> **Lady:** 'How can I change my situation when we have no jobs, no money, no homes and no students and all I feel is grief and loss each day?'

A part of me wanted to agree with her fully and say as much. However, I view the role of a change-agent as being a catalyst for getting the best from people who are in the worst of situations. I offered her the metaphor of the cat and the ball. She listened intently and I finished with the question, 'So which are you?'

> **Lady:** (half-pleading) 'I do not believe I have choice in this situation.'

I reached across to my translator's bottle of water, unscrewed the top and began to throw it over her again. This time she responded by jumping out of her chair and laughing at me.

> **Mike:** 'If you have no choice, then why not stay in the chair and allow me to soak you again?'

She understood the concept that I was attempting to impart and sat down, nodding in thought. I motioned one more time towards throwing some more water at her, just to drive the point home.

> **Lady:** 'STOP' she shouted, half-amused, half-angry.
> **Mike:** 'That's much more like it. I think you have a right to be pissed off at a lot of things right now. So how about you put aside your helplessness and make a plan?'
> **Lady:** 'What sort of a plan? Will you help me build a new school?'
> **Mike:** 'No I won't, but lots of organisations are already beginning to and it won't be too long before you are needed as a teacher once again. Tell me, what stops you from teaching the kids in the camp?'
> **Lady:** 'I have mentioned it to some children and parents at times, but right now people are more in need of essentials like food, shelter, medicine and water. And it is difficult to get the children in one place at the same time.'

My aim was to find a small way to enable this lady to interact meaningfully with kids so that her teaching skills could begin to surface and be used again. I made a suggestion.

Mike: 'What about getting the kids together for a singing class?'

Lady: 'Many of the children go to the [makeshift] churches for this, so it is unlikely that I could get enough of them to join me.'

Mike: 'What do the kids really need?'

Lady: 'Food, water, clothes, vitamins, showers.'

Mike: 'What about clean teeth?'

Lady: 'Of course, but toothbrushes and paste are expensive and not easy to find.'

On my stopover from Miami, I had re-read the message from a nurse friend in Haiti. She had given me a checklist of supplies to bring in. In Miami, I had cleared the local K-Mart of toys, deflated soccer balls and every last toothbrush they had in stock – nearly a hundred in total, along with an equal number of tubes of toothpaste. I reached into the enormous plastic supply box that sat in my tent and gathered all the toothbrushes and toothpaste. With a cheesy grin, I pulled the big bag out and handed it to her.

Mike: 'So, how about you create a teeth-cleaning station at your tent? The kids each have a brush of their own.'

I reached back into the box and pulled out duct tape and marker pen.

Mike: 'And they come to you each day, to use their brush and get a squirt of paste.'

She produced a beautiful wide smile as she took the bag of brushes.

Lady: 'I like this idea very much and so will many of the kids and mothers.'

Naked choice

Take a walk down any busy city street, preferably in a culturally diverse location, and you will not need to look far to appreciate a wide range of skin types, hairstyles, clothing choices, jewellery, body language, physical shapes, walking patterns, talking patterns. In a two-minute walk, you are likely to pass hundreds of individuals who have unique, distinct personalities and who carry unique maps of reality.

List three contexts in which you habitually behave in a predictable fashion.

Some examples from a limitless amount of options are: remaining quiet on public transport, losing your temper when other people aren't doing what you expect of them, drinking alcohol when you get home on a Friday night, pretending you know someone's name when you have forgotten it.

Context 1: _____ Behaviour: _____

Context 2: _____ Behaviour: _____

Context 3: _____ Behaviour: _____

Now, assume that you can change the states you usually experience in these contexts and that you can feel entirely different from how you usually feel.

You could experience joy, confidence, love, enthusiasm, courage or whatever states you desire.

What new behaviours would you choose?

Potential new behaviour 1: _____

Potential new behaviour 2: _____

Despite our own views of the world in the context of this public city street, the majority of us tend to behave in a way that is deemed acceptable by consensus. This is how civilised societies work well much of the time. But in our own moments of street-walking, how many choices are available to us to respond to this environment? You could take your clothes off and walk naked, you could sing and dance along the street, you could lie down in the middle of the pavement and sleep, you could (sin of sins) smile at people as they pass, you could ... the choices are endless. Though we may often respond to our environment in a predictable, controlled fashion, it does not mean we have to.

It's all one

When we take a broader view of our actions in the world, cause/effect as a loop or cycle can be seen to have no difference between initiation (when the cause actually began) and response (when the effect was acted out). Our interactions and communications cannot be divided into parts in any valid way and are all part of one long unit of experience. There are people I have not seen or spoken with in many years, but that does not mean that our relationship has ceased. I may bump into an old friend in the street after 15 years of not seeing him and the relationship continues and has whatever meaning we place upon it after such a long absence.

If you drive a car, you are likely to have encountered at least one traffic jam in your travels. As you join the back of the traffic queue, you see a long line of stopped cars ahead of you. You may be on your way somewhere and be on a tight schedule, such as attending a meeting or appointment, at which point you look at your watch and begin to calculate how late you will be. Most people begin to think of the multiple consequences that accompany missing an appointment and then make judgements on just how good or bad this hold-up will turn out to be.

In many people's map of this experience, turning up late is not their fault, but that of the traffic jam. While you plan alternative appointments, the traffic in front begins to move and you pull forward, changing state as a new hope arises for getting to your destination on time. The traffic then stops again for 20 minutes, which is plenty of time to tense up your muscles and breathing, and create a thousand negative images. This state change is an obvious trigger for at least one response – gritting your teeth and complaining loudly at the view in front of you.

But hallucinate yourself in this or a similar situation now and ask if the stationary traffic is the cause of your lateness? Or is it caused by your decision to take that particular stretch of road? Or was your agreement to meet on this particular day the cause of this lateness? Is the traffic jam, and therefore your potential frustration, due to one of 10,000 other individuals sitting in their cars on this stretch of road? In the same way that we are not individually able to make the traffic flow go faster, the traffic flow is unable to create our thoughts and states inside our vehicle. The 10,000 stationary cars have no way of making us feel anything, as can be seen by some of your fellow car drivers, who seem delighted to be enjoying extra time to listen to a radio show or send a few texts. Yet, for one too many people, the traffic is what is causing them to feel 'angry' and 'stressed'.

No credit, where credit isn't due

One of the reasons I work as a coach is that I get to be a part of some very dramatic and satisfying changes in the lives of the clients I work with. On a number of occasions, clients have informed me that I 'fixed' them, saved them or changed their lives.

When I first started receiving such appreciation I puffed my chest out and gladly soaked up the praise. Then, one day, I was presenting the cause/effect pattern to a client who was good at blaming other people for his problems and I realised that the credit I was so enjoying followed exactly the same line of thinking that I had been suggesting he should avoid.

When a person makes a positive change, with assistance from another, they can still only make those changes themselves. I am far too big to fit into anyone else's neurology and would not have a clue which of the billions of cells to reorganise first. It is not like baking a cake, where I can claim to have made it all by myself. And if you are remaining alert you will jump at the chance to shout – but whose recipe were you using? And who produced the ingredients, and who taught you to bake?

I am not very good at baking, but I often go to great efforts to play with the contexts in a client's life to generate unconscious shifts in their responses to the world. I do my thing, and then the client does his or her thing, which is the majority of the work. Without the other person's engagement and actions, how could there be change? No person's interaction with another can be the cause of the effect; the interactions are simply one part of the whole that enables a person to make the necessary changes inside themselves. With this in mind, I issue a little warning to anyone seeking a guru figure, motivator or leader of any kind to hang his or her hopes and dreams upon. Regardless of the degree of information you receive in the way of ideas or stimulation (such as those provided in this book), you are still the one who has to get up in the morning and run a sequence of thoughts and actions to achieve whatever outcome, or set of outcomes, you are looking for. It is all your responsibility, no matter how lifted up by the words or efforts of another person you may be.

We all know people who excel at communicating great ideas, or even better yet, clear, concise methods to put into action. But as far as I know, no one has ever come along and stepped inside another human being to put out the rubbish, clean their teeth or write a book (shame about this last one). Even my incredible physiotherapist, who has helped me many times with bad climbing injuries, is the first to say that he can manipulate and provoke the injured parts, but the elements of healing and repair are up to me.

What I am really saying is that you, and only you, are the solution you are looking for.

It's all relative

I have smiled with an ironic lip-curl while writing this chapter. As I write, I am currently experiencing the sleep deprivation that can accompany the arrival of a young child, along with multiple late nights of work that are needed to get projects finished.

As the expressions go, I am dog-tired and snowed-under and I can tell that my usual levels of resistance to child chaos courtesy of my two-and-a-half-year-old and his three-year-old cousin (also running riot in our home today), are a little lower than when I sleep more than five hours per night. I have also noticed that I have not exercised for some weeks and may be guilty of using sleep deprivation and work overload as a 'reason' for not doing what I know will benefit me.

Tiredness is currently the dominant state that I am experiencing and I, of course, have the option of dropping some of my work schedule and going to bed for an hour or simply sticking with it. The choice to take a nap exists, but is available only at the cost of falling behind on work and dropping my wife into the chaos of taking care of our kids alone on a hectic weekend.

It strikes me, while in my tired state, that to tell someone, maybe like any struggling, exhausted, single mother, that she always has choice on how to respond, could be deemed insensitive. Tiredness and a multitude of daily stress factors can pick away at our ability to remain resourceful. What I find myself asking in such situations is what the intention is behind my actions and whether I am fulfilling it with my chosen form of response or reaction?

In the case of not exercising recently, my intention is to avoid extra energy expenditure and discomfort (it is the middle of a wet, cold winter and I typically exercise outdoors). However, the consequence is that I miss out on a form of activity that leaves me feeling alert, refreshed and stimulated. As easy as it would be in my tired state to raise my voice at my son for intentionally spraying water over his cousin with the hose pipe (an event that is happening outside the window as I write), he would almost certainly not appreciate or understand my tone for something that, back in the summer, we were experiencing for fun. Added to which I would undermine both my own and my wife's efforts over the last two years to communicate with our son in a respectful manner.

I have just returned from turning off the outside tap, as tight as it will go, and educating the boys on the effects of cold-water soakings in the middle of a freezing winter. 'Okay daddy – whatever.'

I will not take a daytime nap and I have to be accepting of the consequences. This gritty feeling in my eyes is something I cannot change in this immediate moment without taking responsibility for it and choosing a solution. However, just knowing that the nap option exists is enough to free me from thoughts of being at effect from my sleepless nights. My tiredness is presently a given; my response to it is not. We alone are responsible for our states and how we interact with the world we live in, regardless of what happens in the world outside of us.

Even when we seemingly lose all choice over what life presents, it's crucial to remember that our internal response is, and always will be, ours to choose.

CHAPTER 4

FREEDOM FROM
THE EASTER BUNNY

Most people hold beliefs about themselves and the world that influence their behaviour. But all beliefs have a limiting effect by functioning as a prediction and getting in the way of direct experiences. You may hold beliefs you regard as useful, without considering how it is our actions that get us what we want, not those beliefs.

'Frisbeetarianism is the belief that when you die, your soul goes up on the roof and gets stuck.'

George Carlin

I t seems that more than any other processes running through our neurology, beliefs have the strongest influence on the way we live our lives. You will likely know from your own experiences how holding certain beliefs affects who you spend time with, where you live, what you do for a living, how you treat your kids, what you wear, what you eat, how you spend your weekends, how you direct your energy, how you react to world events and pretty much everything that comes your way.

It could be said that there are a lot of positive outcomes of holding beliefs. If you are someone who has a belief that you can always overcome a challenge, such a prediction is more likely to generate positive actions that will support the prediction in coming true. Certainly more than would someone who believes they are incapable of achieving much at all.

The problem with both positions, or indeed all beliefs, is their effect on our choices. Even when we believe that we can overcome a challenge, the fact that we hold such a prediction is, in itself, limiting. How many people have crushed themselves upon the rocks of their convictions when the feedback from the world made it all too clear that their 'can' was in fact a 'cannot'? I am not suggesting a defeatist attitude here, rather flexibility in the way we think. You can still have an optimistic approach to life without having the belief system that holds you into one particular way of thinking and behaving, thereby diminishing some of your choices.

It's common to think that beliefs are required to inhabit our best lives. But that would discount many of the entirely freethinking, open-minded individuals who live successfully in a world of, 'I don't know, but let's have some fun finding out.'

Even when we do 'find out', what becomes our new experience is then only a next level of knowledge and awareness that we can begin to launch new voyages of discovery from. If you take a long look at human existence, current events have pretty much disproved or failed to deliver on every belief that humans could conjure. And it's likely that many of today's facts will become tomorrow's fairytales.

Gnomes in the forest

I've had a number of experiences when younger that generated some strange and convincing beliefs for me. At the time of the following story, I had all the evidence I needed to support what the local indigenous population held to be absolutely true, which was that the jungle I was living in was full of spirits. This experience brought home to me how easy it is to accept even the most bizarre of beliefs and also the descriptions we use to reinforce them.

My new friend was about 18 inches tall, with an impossibly wide mouth and a head the size of a coconut. His ears would have been more at home on a hare and his eyes looked very similar to one of the happier dwarves from the original *Snow White* animation. He transferred to me another intricate secret of the universe, one which I was able to grasp in a conceptual, felt way; meaning there was no chance of actually retelling in any precise, human form a single element of our psychic communication. As we shared that moment under a full moon, deep in the Peruvian Amazon, a thought struck me: 'How weird is it that I don't mind him being next to me while I'm throwing my guts up?' Then I vomited again, making a sound that a companion said triggered images for him of the gates of Hades opening and releasing the garbage that even Hell no longer wanted.

I think it was the eighth or ninth night in a row that I had been seeing these strange little people. There were also enormous giants, coincidentally the size of trees, who would look my way and give me knowing smiles. On one evening the elderly Shipibo shaman, who had been singing and blowing smoke over me and my fellow seekers, looked up and pointed to the same half-human, half-snake-like creature that I knew was hanging from the branch of a tree and watching our ceremony. The old Amazonian wizard looked at me, then to the snake thing and then whispered back to me in Spanish, so that I only caught a few of the words: *'este espíritu es una buena señal, significa la victoria, usted es fuerte, hay no oscuridad'* ('this spirit is a good sign, it means victory, you are strong, no darkness').

My appreciation for this 'victory' was transient, in between bouts of expelling my entire insides. However, even through 'la purga', the name given to the commonly experienced vomit reflex, I was feeling some sense of shamanic, spiritual superiority due to the number of 'spirits' I was meeting and communicating with each night. While few of my friends had even the mildest sniff of a visitation, I hallucinated an entire fairy world that would have given Peter Jackson's CGI team reason to be impressed. The shaman said it best, 'The spirits visit you when you're ready.' He could have also added, 'and anyway, Mike, unlike the others, you've been drinking double the amount of one of the world's strongest-known hallucinogens'.

When I was younger, I had made a number of visits to the Peruvian Amazon for intense periods of learning about indigenous shamanic practices. Some brains are clearly more sensitive to Dimethyltryptamine (DMT) than others and the ability to hallucinate wildly is either dose-dependent or genetically predisposed, or possibly, as in my case, both.

My reasons for visiting the Amazon and taking part in these rituals were many and varied, but predominantly because I had read that the indigenous brew that contains DMT – known as 'ayahuasca' – was like going through 10 years of therapy in one hit. I am a big advocate of short cuts if they are proven to be effective, so drinking a little cup of vine tea in a traditional setting seemed an ideal way to change my spiritual direction and pave the way for life to provide more of what I desired.

Shortly after returning from an Amazon trip, I discussed the shamanic processes with my friend and mentor, John. I mentioned to him some of the more incredible experiences that had taken place while I was in the Amazon.

John: 'What's your intention for drinking it?'
Mike: 'It's viewed by the Indians as medicine for spiritual development.'

John chuckled with a smile, before asking,

John: 'Funny, I've still not encountered a person who can specify for me what the word *spiritual* means?'

I assumed he was asking because he wanted confirmation that I knew the importance of the term.

Mike: 'It's a connection with God or the universe, or whatever is out there.'
John: (still with a wry smile on his face) 'So, what you're saying is that if it's a connection, it's actually a feeling or a state?'

I had a feeling I was being enticed into a wrestling match by someone five weight classes above my own.

Mike: 'Yes, it's a feeling and also a way of living.'

John: 'So it's a feeling and also a strategy or pattern of behaviours?'

I hesitated, before stating,

Mike: 'Yes, and it's knowing that there is more to life than what we can see.'

John: 'How?'

Mike: 'How what?'

Mike: 'How do you know there's more than you can see?'

Mike: 'Well,' I replied tentatively, 'because I feel it when I meditate, or pray, or have little moments like déjà vu, and anyway, I have seen it, as real as I see you right now. After drinking ayahuasca in the Amazon, I saw through what was like a veil to this other world that was as real and clear as this one.'

John: 'Next time you go into that world, do you think you could bring back a physical object?'

Mike: 'Sure, I'll see what I can get.'

In the walls of this particular reality tunnel, cracks began to appear.

I suspect that many readers of a book such as this are interested in evidence of some kind. You may or may not be someone who considers yourself to be religious or spiritual; however, I am guessing that you hold at least some form of belief about either yourself or an aspect of life. The challenge that was given to me during the above conversation was one that I realised held far more importance and relevance than the subject of plant-induced hallucinations.

I thought for a moment about what the term 'spiritual' really meant to me and invite you to take a moment to do the same.

My own – until then – unchallenged view had been developed from reading numerous books on Native American culture, shamanism and Buddhism. I regularly practised meditation and yoga and viewed both as a cooler route than traditional religion for connecting with the unseen and possibly getting a place in heaven or shooting up the karmic pyramid.

My teacher questioned me a second time:

John: 'So, tell me specifically what the word *spiritual* means to you?'

I thought about it before answering.

Mike: 'If and when I assume to feel "spiritually connected", through whatever activity I engage in, then that is simply a feeling or state. Feelings are not distinct, objective experiences, they're nebulous, subjective sensations that exist as an orchestra of electrical and chemical reactions in our neurology. If I aim to live a spiritual life, by way of practising certain value-based decisions and actions, I'm simply choosing to engage differently to my environment than others, or indeed similarly to other spiritually minded/engaged people. And if spirituality is simply a belief in something I cannot see, hear, touch, taste or smell, then, well, I'm just exercising blind faith without the slightest shred of evidence.'

From our location that day in the Santa Cruz Mountains the penny of my realisation could be heard dropping all the way back to the coast.

In the language that you and I use, no word or statement has any inherent meaning beyond what we attach to it. This is not only relevant for words, but also for everything else around us. We humans are meaning-making machines, adept at making meaning out of everything we encounter, even though almost none of that meaning is in the experience itself, but rather in the belief structure behind our interpretation of the experience.

Wrong assumptions

One of my very busy female executive clients, Alice, complained recently of a phone call she had received. At weekends Alice gives her family most of her attention. She answered the telephone to her elderly grandmother in the middle of cooking lunch for five people. Alice hurriedly told her grandmother she would call back later as she was so busy. Her grandmother groaned in a familiar tone, 'Okay, you don't care about what I have to say anyway.'

Alice groaned herself, 'If only Gran could have seen the bold letters already written that morning at the top of my to-do list, reminding me to call her that day. It had only been three days since we had last spoken, after all.'

Alice's grandmother's ability to make her own meaning from statements is hardly unique to her. 'I will call you back later as I'm busy right now' was interpreted to mean, 'You don't care about what I have to say.'

Consider what assumptions Granny had to make to believe that her busy granddaughter does not care about what she has to say.

As far as her Gran could actually know, Alice's need to call her back may have been because she wanted to have more time to hear what Gran had to say. It could be because her kids were about to set the house on fire. Alice could have been desperate for the bathroom or, simply, as was the actual case, in the middle of feeding her hungry family.

You can generate thousands (more precisely, an infinite set) of other sets of conditions that would 'explain' Alice's preference to call back later. Taking the context into account is all-important as on one day you make a certain correct assumption, but on another day have a completely different understanding of exactly the same situation. Hence Alice's grandmother's selection of this particular interpretation had zero justification whatsoever. Something she most likely forgot when Alice called her back for a 40-minute chat about nothing much after that lunch.

Other examples of our interpretation/meaning-making processes could be:

1. **'You come home late, therefore you don't care about me'**
   Despite the fact that the person coming home late is working her backside off to support her lazy partner, or happens to work so far away from home that the chances of getting back before 8pm are non-existent when leaving at a normal end-of-business time.
2. **'He's overweight and has stopped paying attention to his health'**
   Actually, the dude is preparing for an Arctic crossing on skis and needs all the extra blubber he can hold.

3. **'The latest employment numbers clearly show that we are the only political party to run this country'**
   Even though the rise in employment has been a minor increase on the many that were lost when your party took control, what about all that other stuff like major cuts to education, services, health? Oh, and there are other parties.

Problems arise when we hastily interpret and make meaning of what other people say and do. With our own filters in place to bias our view, we can rarely experience anything resembling the real intentions of others. You may recognise in yourself a tendency to judge yourself by your intentions but to judge others only by what you observe in their actions. As an example, one of my friends commented how, as an awkward teenager, she never received any cards or attention on Valentine's Day. After a couple of years of this her mother decided to make her daughter feel better. So she sent her daughter an anonymous card and flowers, which lifted the young girl's spirits with intrigue. A week or so later, when arguing with her brother over some trivial matter, he let slip the truth of her unknown admirer. My friend was furious, upset and humiliated. She interpreted her mother's actions as being underhand and patronising. Her mother's actual intention was to give her daughter a little lift in self-esteem and to feel attractive. But as happens all too often, the meaning was made from the actions, not the good intentions of the mother.

If we fail to seek clarity in what we experience or avoid asking what other people's intentions are, we miss out on important opportunities to communicate at a more precise level. This can often lead to assigning false beliefs, generalisations and distortions where there may be little validity for such things.

Next time you are confused, upset or unsettled by someone else's actions, simply ask that person what their intentions are behind what they're doing. You'll find that this simple question can save you the trouble of jumping to the wrong conclusions and provide more clarity to your communication with others.

THE SUBJECT OF MEANING

The intention of this little experiment is to experience how easily we each make meaning and to realise how subjective that meaning is.

Make no meaning

1. Take a 10-minute walk and notice any number of small events, such as a bird flying across your path, people walking past you without making eye contact, wind blowing in the trees, a type of car going by. Make a mental note of what meaning you usually make from these events.

2. Adopt a Second Position of someone who has an entirely different world-view to you. Now review those same events/experiences again and compare how you might make an entirely new set of meanings for each one. You could watch the bird as a person who is an ornithologist or has a phobia of birds. You could take a mechanic's position when the car goes by. When a person ignores you in the street you could adopt a position of someone who is desperate for attention.

3. Adopt a number of different Second Positions, such as a priest, doctor, president of the USA, a member of the opposite sex, and give meaning to events through those filters. Repeat this until you realise how subjective your own meaning-making views are.

It can be good to spend an entire day (or lifetime) experiencing life as directly as possible, and without rushing to interpret every little event.

If wars start, if bosses give you a hard time, if partners shout, if black cats cross your path, no matter what happens, just state what the event is in precise, sensory-based terms, 'the boss is grumbling', and then leave it at that until you have enough information to really know what is on your boss's mind, for example.

Take action

There is little doubt that random, unexpected events, or going on strange adventures, possibly even to the Amazon, can act as catalysts for change in our lives, setting some of us on a very different path from the ones we were on before. However regardless of how profound such events may be, their usefulness can best be measured by the degree to which we utilise the experience, as is evident in the following story.

A 50-year-old client, James, came to me and complained that he had been on a number of very expensive and well-known business training courses to help him move his business forward. He owned a vintage clothing store that had traded extremely well for a period but was now in major downturn. James had spent thousands of pounds on a business training/ marketing course and had come away motivated and certain it would work for him. A month or so after the course, however, he was now convinced that the economy was wrong for his particular offering to the market and that he had wasted his time and money and would soon lose his shop.

I asked him about the content of the business training he had attended and it sounded as though it was of a really high quality, with specific strategies for turning his business around.

I asked him if he had kept in contact with any of the other course attendees and if he knew of any who had used their training successfully. He mentioned two people. I then asked him to call the one who was likely to be doing best. We called and got through to a lady who owned a small food-delivery company in London. I explained the purpose of the call and she laughed and said she was happy to answer my questions on loudspeaker for James.

My first question was simply, 'What from the training worked for you?' Her answer was 'everything'. I then asked *how* it had made such a difference? What followed was a 20-minute summary of the business training that both she and James had attended, put into action by her, step by step, as it was presented to them in their teaching presentations and electronic manuals. She had utilised all of the strategies she had been taught and was seeing the benefits. After telling us about her new processes and the amount of extra business it was generating, she asked James a question: 'How many of the marketing methods have you followed up on, James? I haven't seen you asking questions on the forum or Facebook page at all.'

James's reply said it all. 'I really believe in the approach we learned. I just don't have the desire to make it happen.'

We can believe in things all day long, but unless we utilise our experiences in the real world of actions, there is little chance of getting the results we desire. James actually concluded that he was utterly bored of selling clothes and no matter how much the strategies might work for his business he did not have the enthusiasm for putting any of them in place.

We don't need to believe in anything to get what we want from life as long as we are committed to taking action, and I invite you to consider that living without beliefs of any kind is a far superior way to inhabit our world.

I don't believe it

Clearly it is a rare person who has no beliefs and for some it may even seem impossible, let alone desirable, to drop them all. Existing without beliefs goes against a lot of what we are taught about how to get the best from life.

Examples such as:

- 'You need to believe in yourself, no matter what.'
- 'If you don't believe in yourself, then how can you expect to get what you want from life?'
- 'Self-belief is the breakfast of champions.'
- 'To achieve your dreams requires belief and faith in yourself.'
- 'Ye who have little faith.'
- 'Belief in a life worth living will create it.'

Then there are the really common ones, such as 'it's meant to be', 'it's not meant to be', 'that's karma', 'everything will be fine/okay when the planets align', and my favourite: 'science has the answers', though admittedly I've never heard an actual scientist make that claim.

Can we really expect to achieve optimum positive results unless we believe in ourselves to some degree?

Take time out to observe any successful person you know, or know of, and throughout their typical day they, like you, will follow certain patterns of actions and behaviours. A long-term client of mine is an extremely accomplished businessman who owns a number of large online entertainment platforms. His net worth is in the hundreds of millions and he has thousands of employees working for his family in multiple countries. He considers himself a religious person, who was married in a Catholic church. He fasts a week for Lent and sings Christmas carols when it is that time of year. His two kids are baptised and he tells me that he prays and gives thanks every night of the week for everything that he has. He is genuinely grateful that his version of God has given him so many blessings in material form.

He also happens to be one of the most ambitious, focused and driven individuals I know. He is often taking calls from multiple time zones late at night and early into the morning. He is ruthless at setting performance targets with his senior management teams and insists that everyone in the creative and strategy sector of his business studies the competition on a daily basis. He works 12 to 14 hours a day, religiously. Holding his attention at lunch is a challenge, with two phones glowing in front of him.

Would he be less or more successful without his beliefs?

If he is able to execute the same actions each day without his beliefs, then he is likely to achieve the same results. It is highly unlikely that his faith in a particular form of God is in any way causative to his success, otherwise there would never be any successful atheists, and all of the pious, devout poor people might experience a little more material blessing.

But would my client be as driven or committed to his success without his faith?

Unless he is willing to drop his beliefs for a long enough test period (he is not, I have challenged him with it) we can never know the answer to this last question.

There is little doubt that for some people they can use their beliefs to create a sense of certainty and congruency. The majority of individuals I have met serving in disaster zones have a belief in serving a higher power. Would they do so without that belief in place? Only the individual can answer to his or her own true motives and if the end result is a positive one I, personally, would not care much who you are doing it for. But I have met people who do good deeds out of fear of otherwise sizzling on a bed of coals. That is the equivalent to me of working in a job I hate every day just because it makes me a lot of money.

What we can be certain of is that beliefs are in no way singularly responsible for the outcomes we might achieve. The credit for all outcomes resides firmly with the actions my friend produces. From the moment he wakes, he is down to business. Nothing in the material world can take form unless action happens, despite what you may be led to believe about laws of attraction and visualising what you want, rather than getting off your backside and working for it.

Don't believe me?

Sit for the next month and do nothing but visualise, thinking only about what you want. You could also speak to the universe and recite precisely what it is that you desire out of life. At no point should you leave your house or interact with anyone else. This is about sending the strongest, clearest message to the cosmos without any interference from bothersome tasks like work and paying the bills. Is anyone crazy enough to do that?

That is not to say that visualising what you want is not a partially effective way to direct your neurology towards appropriate actions, it's just that that word 'action' has to be at the forefront of all such strategies.

Is a belief just a belief?

Have you ever stopped to consider what is actually going on with the type of thoughts and feelings that we call 'beliefs'?

I had never given much thought to the structure of my own beliefs. A linguist offered me a description:

'Beliefs are the imposing of meaning upon an event that hasn't happened yet. They're potentially limiting and corruptive because they're decisions made about what will happen or what something will mean prior to actually having the experience in question, thereby guaranteeing that if you are wrong (nearly always except for trivial examples), those beliefs will filter out precisely the set of experiences that would otherwise serve as counter-examples and correct the nonsense contained in the belief.'

> 'Toto, I've a feeling we're not in Kansas anymore' (Dorothy in The Wizard of Oz)

Think about it, if what you believe can be seen, heard, touched, smelled, tasted, or, more likely, a combination of these inputs, then it's not a belief, it's evidence of something tangible. For us to carry beliefs we have to be happy to use a large amount of blind faith and also live with an ongoing degree of prediction, so pass the crystal ball, Tarot cards and tea leaves while you are at it. Beliefs, after all, have not happened yet in a form that can be verified. They exist only in the internal world of the believer and that can be a very dangerous position to be in, as I have encountered many times.

'Mike, a voodoo curse has been cast on you. The priest who was working with Bronte is mad that you gave her new spells. Be very careful, you are being attacked. The priest says bad things will happen to you.'

The lovely Marie, who was providing me with this warning, was deeply sincere as she conveyed concerns for my safety.

Mike: 'Is this priest coming up here to get me?' I asked in a sarcastic tone.

Marie: 'You must take this seriously, Mike, he's powerful.'

Mike: 'Well, I doubt he's about to come up here and take on the UN troops at the perimeter fence any day soon, so his spell had better be accurate. And anyway, what's meant to happen to me? Will I turn into a frog or fall pregnant?'

Marie laughed and scolded me with a tut and a headshake.

Marie: 'You're crazy, man. Ha – fall pregnant, that's funny!'

I was now a target for voodoo curses, a claim that I will remain proud of for the rest of my life.

Three days earlier in Haiti, a 25-year-old woman had come to our medical triage complaining of crawling sensations under her skin, due to what she believed to be a powerful curse placed upon her. 'Bronte' had been paying for some spells to counter the curse but could no longer afford them. She had not eaten or slept well for days and was a rare sight in her filthy clothes and unkempt hair. I signalled to my translator to close all of the tent flaps so that no one could see in. I then instructed Vanessa explicitly that she was to keep a very serious tone throughout my interaction with this young woman. I was told that Bronte had been experiencing an itching feeling for a number of weeks and when she went to the local voodoo priest he told her that she had a bad demon under her skin. One that would require a lot of regular charms and spells to be bought from him to resolve the issue, all at a price, of course.

Bronte, like many young Haitians, has grown up in a culture that accepts a belief in spirits and entities existing among the living and exerting control over the lives of those who fall foul of their spell. Luckily, voodoo spirits are not all bad and if you happen to find yourself having a good run of luck or positive results you can hand the credit for your success over to any number of heavenly candidates too.

I had read a book on voodoo before landing in Haiti as I suspected that I would encounter at least one person believing they were possessed or cursed. Despite my personal experiences from three trips to the Amazon and some pretty mind-blowing meditation retreats, I remain firmly agnostic regarding the existence of any spirits or things that go bump in the night. Though it would be my tendency to now disbelieve in any such phenomena, I guard against the trap of believing that not believing is not a belief, meaning (mine at least) that if we assume the world to be entirely as we experience it now, through our limited sensory apparatus, we also fall dangerously into an absolute position from which we filter out new evidence.

The old-school, unbiased-by-commercial-interests, process of scientific discovery seems to be a fine way of describing and appreciating nature in its observable forms. But it is not as if science is exempt from beliefs. Many an erring researcher has used the word 'proof' when presenting their results, despite the fact that far too many scientific theories prior to the current ones have been disproven over the years.

Scientific practice seems best viewed as a provisional investigation that pushes and prods what we can currently understand but never hold as 'truth'.

Most logical, analytical thinkers have a whole host of objections to the majority of stories and tenets that form the basis of religions. But a truly open and curious mind surely has to acknowledge its own limitations. Hence, I question how anyone can so easily accept, without evidence, that there absolutely is not some 'thing' or 'doing', or maybe 'thingdoing', that exists beyond our knowledge or ability to ever comprehend. Having no current experience of an event or thing does not mean it does not exist.

It does seem puzzling that in a universe as vast as ours, a creative thingdoing would even bother to attempt imparting and imposing club rules to a bunch of evolving monkeys, in a communication form, such as language, that is so open to interpretation and misrepresentation that even a three-year-old can find flaws in it. It simply does not add up, regardless of what branding you attempt to rework or wrap it in.

Being cautiously open-minded seems to be a smart approach for anyone who is scientifically/curiously compelled. If good science/curiosity practice means being open to being proven wrong in our own findings and always seeking new evidence to the contrary of our current understanding, then how could an intelligent thinker take any other position? And if the scientific method is the best we currently have, it is surely a good idea to become like an effective scientist in our daily activities and gladly admit when we're wrong or in need of updating our positions. With this in mind, every single line in this book is to be scrutinised because I am all too aware of how ignorant I am of everything I am currently ignorant of.

Back in Haiti, I asked my translator to explain to the 'possessed' Bronte that I fully appreciated her problem. As an aside from working with psychological methods, I was trained to work with the evil spirits surrounding her, by using magic I had learned from the shamans on my Amazonian visits. I qualified this last point by revealing a tattoo on my stomach that is alleged to be a power symbol used by ancient Mayan healers. A friend pointed out that it could, in fact, be a symbol for the public toilets back in the day.

Bronte was convinced of my status as shown in her wider-than-previous eyes and an agitated shift in her breathing and position on the chair, as she sat way back, in an attempt to get as far away from me as possible. This young woman was so traumatised by the constant manipulation at the hands of the local 'priest' that I could have easily shown her a frog and convinced her it was a prince. However, informing her that what she was experiencing was a consequence of her neurons firing ineffectively would have most likely lost me the opportunity to assist her. Though I might not subscribe personally to the beliefs of my clients, I still aim to step into their reality long enough to appreciate it before moving them forward.

For approximately 10 minutes I chanted, sprayed a little water over Bronte, rolled my eyes and throughout this theatrical display, I coached her through the unconscious reframing pattern, 'Aligning with the unconscious' as detailed in Chapter 5 (Freedom from one mind) all cloaked in a little freshly acquired voodoo terminology. After completing the steps of the process and finishing with a flourish of Tibetan chanting that I had learned years earlier on a meditation retreat, Bronte was breathing evenly and had lost all of the previous tension in her face and torso. Her eyes no longer looked as though they were being held open and her constant hand-fidgeting had stopped. I quietly waited and allowed this new state to settle for a few minutes before speaking.

Mike: 'Bronte, we just used good magic to clear away the bad. These curses and spells can have no more effect over you, do you understand?'

She nodded, but with hesitation.
I asked her to voice her concerns.

Bronte: 'I feel, better, but I am worried that another spirit or curse will attack me again.'

I ventured a question in return.

Mike: 'Do you know what these curses and spirits feed on?'

She shook her head, 'No'.
I became serious, in part because anger would be an appropriate response to the scumbags who trap young people into believing that their 'magic' is the saviour to real-life challenges.

Mike: 'There is only one thing that dark spirits or curses need to feed on you and affect you, and that *is your belief in them.*'

As she processed this statement, I added:

Mike: 'These spirits and curses become more powerful when you give them strength with your belief.' I pointed at my translator, 'This is possibly why Vanessa here has never been attacked or harmed by voodoo, because she doesn't give these things any power, she doesn't believe in them and therefore they cannot feed on her.'

Bronte nodded in realisation at the simplicity of what I was saying.

I continued:

Mike: 'I am here for two more weeks. You can visit me anytime, but the magic we just used does not require that you believe in it. In fact, it is better that you forget all about it. What I would like you to do now is to promise me you will give no more power to these spirits. For the next two weeks, if you think of them, I want you to make the pictures of them really small and place them in little boxes, to be forgotten about. If you get any of the bad feelings at all, simply use the same steps we just went through to change those feelings. Your beliefs feed these curses and I want you to starve them.'

In Bronte's case, you might say, 'Hold up, she believed and also had evidence for her problem – her skin crawled and she felt like she was going to die' (some, in the West, would call these panic attacks). Except Bronte's belief in spirits could never be confirmed as the cause of the states that were ruining her life. She did not need to believe that she had physiological responses because she had direct and painful evidence for them. However her beliefs regarding the source of her problems were merely add-ons to the reality of her experience. Her symptoms were verifiable, but spirits and curses as a source might require some time before they are confirmed, if ever.

We know that there are many elements surrounding us that we do not experience with any degree of conscious recognition. Subatomic particles pass through each of us every second of the day and yet we fail to register their existence. Radio waves and Wi-Fi fill our environment, but we require technological interfaces to know that they exist and to utilise their effects. So maybe there are some voodoo spirits dancing on the shoulders of unfortunate Haitians. If that is true, they are very effectively dealt with by using entirely non-belief-based methods, and, hey, maybe it is purely a coincidence that people who do not believe in demons or possessions do not get troubled by them.

My bunny is bigger than yours

If you think about another person's belief system, that believer tends to present his or her belief as being more prominent than anyone else's. It's often competitive, a divide that is a major factor in dispute, war, unrest and terrorism.

When the Twin Towers went down in New York, I watched the live news with two friends. At the time in New York City we all had friends working in the area of the attacks. I remember all of us sitting in stunned dread, until one friend spoke up, 'This is the most horrific thing I have ever seen in my life.' Meanwhile, among many of the believers of Jihad, there was great celebration at the loss of innocent lives.

It is clear that meaning isn't inherent in the world, but is something we each create, based on our beliefs and whichever reality tunnel we choose (or not) to live inside. For us, to hold beliefs requires that we make meaning about events and experiences that have not happened yet, and to disallow any new information that comes in to counter such beliefs.

So what is so bad about that?

The drawbacks of this form of thinking are:

- If I believe that the reason I did not get the job was because it was not 'meant to be', how am I going to learn from the experience and work out how I can improve before my next interview?
- If I believe that all people of a certain race are to be mistrusted, how will that affect my relationships with people who are different from me?
- If I believe that all poor people are lazy, how will this affect my actions towards others who are less well off than me?
- If I believe that children should be seen and not heard, what will my family experiences be like?
- If I believe that I am superior to others, where does my compassion go?

- If I believe that I am totally awesome and capable of turning anything I touch into gold, how do I process my failures? Does my deep self-belief then require me to point the blame elsewhere, because I am infallible?

Many people know the dangers of this last form of belief. A number of the teenagers I work with who have stated that they have confidence issues, grow up in environments that knock the hell out of any sense of self-esteem they might otherwise develop. Their environments provide an assault of challenges from adults who take the position of always being right about everything, despite the adults lacking the intelligence to seek actual evidence for what they claim.

One of my young mentees stated that, 'My dad has never once admitted his f*ck-ups or wrongdoings after pushing his bullshit on us every day. If he did it would come with blame attached for what we made him do.' If individuals like 'dad' were to put aside their cast-iron belief in their own infallibility just long enough to seek evidence for their part in the family's troubles, we might see a lot more harmony being created.

I invite you, for a moment, to entertain the idea of everyone on the planet being willing to put their beliefs aside just long enough to experience other ways of viewing the world. What effect would it have if you woke every day and challenged yourself to disprove what you currently believe to be true about life?

Your beliefs may be really important to you – or not. Some people go their whole lives without ever challenging what they have learned to accept from the earliest of ages. Are you curious and adventurous enough to wonder what would happen if you stopped believing anything for a day and, instead, asked yourself over and over again,

'How do I know this is true and what verifiable evidence do I have to support it?'

Remain flexible

There is an enormous uprooted oak tree at the back of our home. The last time some major winds came through these parts the tree went over after a few hundred years of life. When I look at all the smaller, bushier, trees around it, they seem to have suffered no such effect. Unlike the oak, the younger trees bend, move, sway and flex with ease against whatever pushes them. It is a great reminder to me to remain flexible in the positions I take, though admittedly some people seem very capable of holding firm in their beliefs, despite a tornado-worth of counter-evidence, as might be viewed in examples such as climate-change deniers or people who believe that genetics dictate our behaviours. Both beliefs that simply require a glimmer of intelligence use to dispel.

That is not to say that we should not take our own positions on subjects that we have experience of or can source evidence for.

For example, I have an absolute, cast-iron position on violence towards children. I aim to remain flexible in most of my views, but no degree of counter-evidence (I doubt that any exists beyond opinion) could persuade me that physically hitting or verbally humiliating a child of any age could ever be an effective form of teaching/parenting.

Is that a belief? In my reality, there is a vast amount of evidence that shows such reactions to children only have a negative effect. But there are many people who might disagree and tell me that a short, sharp smack has the effect of reordering disorder in their kids and that they have plenty of evidence to show for it.

I've been accused of believing that eating healthily is important (to which I refer to hundreds of studies as evidence); that experiences are more rewarding than owning excess stuff (there are some studies, but personal experience and observation can support this one pretty clearly); that working most of our lives for money rather than for satisfaction is a losing game (do you know anyone who can disprove this?); that governments should have less control over individual choices (where is the barcode on my body that says, 'I am property'?); that birds should not be kept in cages (have you seen how fast and high they can fly?); that psychiatry has had its time (unless it's willing to step out of the dark ages of medicating behavioural problems and evolve); that art, music and dance are as important as maths and grammar in education (just ask any artist, musician or dancer).

Are these beliefs?

I do not currently regard them as such. For me, they are temporary operational guides, open to challenge and revision by further experience in the knowledge that life is organic and constantly in the process of change, so why shouldn't thoughts and beliefs be equally open to change too?

Take a look at yourself

You might notice that it is in the subjects we feel strongest about that we are less likely to seek counter-examples. Some people reject evidence against their beliefs so strongly that it reinforces their view, regardless of how clear that evidence is. But what the believer is really presenting is their need to be right about the subject matter.

My question is: what's so good about being right all the time?

Being 'right' may keep us in the same holding pattern of feeling secure and superior, but it leaves little room for new experiences, learning and development. Deliberately challenging the assumptions and beliefs we hold about ourselves and the world could well be the quickest and most rewarding route to freedom of the kind that allows us to be who we really want to be.

When we accept beliefs in any form, we are then open to accept the beliefs of others. I do not know about you, but knowing how flawed my own map of reality has been over the years only makes me more suspicious of the maps of those around me, especially anyone who claims to have THE MAP or THE TRUTH or any inside scoop on life, which must be followed in order to find heaven, social stability, happiness or a million bucks. This suspicion thoroughly applies to this book and any statement made by me. Believe none of it. Accept none of it. Test, test, test all of it, should you be curious enough to put in the time towards doing so.

> 'Living in someone else's reality tunnel is Hell. Living in your own is heaven.'
>
> Robert Anton Wilson

I would add to that,

> 'Living with no fixed reality tunnel at all avoids notions of heaven and hell, and puts you squarely into the action of life as it really happens (almost)!'

For those of you who may find this assault on your beliefs to be offensive, uncomfortable, or both: good. I am succeeding at doing my job with this book, and ... please relax. It's not my role to be chief executioner of all the fairies, ogres, Easter bunnies and Santa. I'm offering these views so that you have the choice to believe or not. There seem to be few benefits in being mindlessly indoctrinated into certain ways of thinking without having an alternative perspective. Carry beliefs if they work for you, but ensure you at least know about some of the many ideas that run counter to what you're committing yourself.

Living without any beliefs may seem challenging to some, but can provide a number of beneficial effects. These effects could be named 'freedom' and 'choice' from limiting beliefs about who you are and what you're capable of.

If you have ever stated any of the following, you will know these limitations in your own beliefs:

- 'I can't do it'
- 'I'm not good enough'
- 'My actions won't have any effect'
- 'I can't make a difference'

- 'It's not my responsibility'
- 'I'm a victim'
- 'I don't have his/her looks/talent/skills'
- 'I'm not worthy'
- 'Good stuff happens to other people'
- 'Life is difficult'
- 'People are bad/stupid/untrustworthy'
- 'It's not meant to be'

Being belief-free, or at least flexible enough to drop them when necessary, enables a freedom to make choices upon a simple formula: will the choices you make and the actions arising from those choices have the positive consequences that you desire?

It is a liberating experience to have no absolute fixed position on how your life *must, should* or *ought* to be lived in a particular fashion, style or ideal.

You will still have your own preferences towards how you spend your allotted time on earth, which will likely evolve and change over the coming years too. But at least being belief-free might keep you more open to learning new ideas, taking unlikely opportunities and diving into new experiences.

On a bigger scale, and as a father, I sometimes allow myself to dream of my sons growing up in a world free of beliefs. Imagine, for a moment, the peace we might experience if every person sought evidence for his or her assumptions? Imagine if politicians and decision-makers acknowledged that their wars and policies stemmed from ignorance of the limitations of their own perceptions, their need to be right and their thinking with superiority. When we stop believing in the interpretations and meaning we make about our experiences and clean up the act of such beliefs, we might take fewer gambles and make fewer errors from the belief that our reality, and our culture's reality, is *the best reality*.

As if!

I don't believe a word of it

If your beliefs serve you well (how would you know unless you have dropped them long enough to experience the counter?), then please ignore everything you have just read. Or, in fact, believe that it was written because the author is aligned with an indecisive force that is attempting to take over the world and turn everyone into non-believers for the purpose of working in an agnostic factory, churning out fences to sit on.

Dropping our beliefs requires an honesty and degree of humility that many of us are not familiar with and would find hugely challenging. To become open-minded to being 'wrong' may be essential for a genuine intelligent approach to life. Ironically, I have caught myself believing that being open-minded is the smartest position to hold. When it comes down to the binary choice of believer or non-believer, there is only 'I know', meaning I do know that I believe or I do know that I don't believe. Either position contains a certainty that will likely overlap from one subject to others.

When we're certain in one context, we're likely to make the same error of certainty in others and potentially miss out on all that counter-information available to us.

Maybe this explains how and why so many people believe that it is normal to experience stressful, unhappy, boring, dreary, monotonous and hopeless visions of the world. When at all times the counter-example is right there in front of us.

Ultimately, beliefs are no more than choices that act like filters through which to experience the world. For some, to live without those filters is to take away the flavour from a favourite ice cream. The distinction I propose is to at least know that your flavour is not the only flavour that runs through the cream and that there are other ingredients not even related to the taste at all. Indeed, in some cases, the flavours are so artificial as to not have a single element of chocolate, mint, strawberry, or whatever, in them. It is all fake-believe.

I have a personal suspicion that it's unlikely that anything in our lives is absolute (just, maybe, including death), or that things are meant to be and that this is what the universe wants.

Almost everything you desire within the laws of physics is within the scope of your own abilities to make happen and, hopefully, someone will change the laws of physics, so disproving this last statement.

To have freedom, we require choice. Choose your beliefs if you must carry such creations, but choose them wisely.

CHAPTER 5

FREEDOM FROM ONE MIND

We each experience life through the conscious and unconscious mind. When these two levels of consciousness are misaligned we often experience unwanted consequences. When they are aligned we are more likely to achieve our best. States/feelings and the majority of behaviours arise from the unconscious, which can be our worst enemy or greatest ally.

'Out beyond ideas of wrong doing and right doing, there is a field. I'll meet you there.'

Mevlana Jelaluddin Rumi, 13th-century mystic

S ome years ago, I used to climb difficult rock faces without ropes. When I was just turning 20, I travelled all the way to Australia from England with a goal of climbing a famous, large overhanging rock face without any safety equipment, so that I could hang from one hand, 30 metres above the ground in ice-cool fashion.

Like many climbers and extreme-sport athletes that ascend through the ranks of dangerous events, I learned – by the skin of my teeth and trial and error – to move into, embrace and utilise the body sensations of adrenaline that came from my sport. Fear was often more of an ally than an enemy because I had learned to appreciate that with the increase of potent biochemicals came extra strength, decreased reaction lag, time distortion and hyper-alertness.

However, as I stood at the bottom of the climb I had travelled all the way to Australia for, my blasé exterior hid an uncomfortable sensation that had started on the walk towards it. It was not fear, but it certainly was not enthusiasm or confidence either. Unlike most other times in my life when I respond to my unconscious needs and will often eat only minutes before dinner to satisfy a sudden hunger, or nap in the middle of a busy workplace to top up on lost sleep, at the foot of my climb I chose to ignore a set of signals that were arising in my body.

I climbed up an easy vertical bottom section of the wall while still feeling the unusual discomfort. I arrived at the apex where the vertical wall meets a horizontal roof at 30 metres above a very hard rocky ground. I looked out across the line of holds that would lead me, upside down, to the lip, where I intended to hang one-handed with a serene look upon my face. As I reached out to the first large hold, what would usually have been a fluid, confident movement, with no tension, became a pause, mid-stretch. My muscles did not want to follow through the motion of leaving one hold and gaining the next, despite my conscious intent. For a split second, it struck me as odd that I would feel the brakes going on without me pressing the pedal. After all, was I not the operator of the vehicle?

I awkwardly moved into an entirely upside-down position. My feet left the vertical back wall and I hooked my right heel into the crack I was holding on to. I eyed the next handhold, which was big by my standards of climbing. I stretched for it again and felt the same rubber-band resistance. My arm just did not want to extend to the next move. Sweat began pouring off me and uncomfortable sensations fired off in my chest.

Climbing is a sport in which you notice a severe drop in strength and fitness after only two weeks of not practising it. By the time I had arrived at this point, upside down and sweating, I had not climbed for nearly two months. Which, as any fool will tell you, is not the time to attempt free soloing, way above the ground and upside down, on a horizontal roof. However, my stubborn conscious commitment to reach the lip of this climb paid off. Through sweat, hesitant moves and a set of chest-thumping alarm-bell sensations, I found myself at the lip of this world-famous rock route that I had dreamed of climbing for years. Except that my dream of arriving ice cool and serene was very different from the reality.

My arms were now flooded with lactic acid and I could feel the numbness in my hands that usually heralds the imminent release from the rock. Salt stung my eyes and my mouth was resonating with the metallic taste of pure fear. I was shaking, panting and so desperately tired that I was unable to take one hand off to reach the next hold.

Had I been tied to a rope, I would have let go a full minute before, just to relieve the pain of the acid build-up in my arms. But I could not choose to let go, other than with one hand, to find the next hold. I looked around frantically to find what I might be missing. When no miracle solution appeared, I did what normally spells out a fatal result – I looked down to see the ground below me.

No peace or sense of acceptance came with viewing my final resting ground. I remember my conscious mind screaming quite clearly, 'I've blown it, I'm dead, I'm fucking dead.' And then, to make matters comprehensively worse, my foot popped off from under the roof, so that all my weight dropped onto my arms in a pull-up position. My last thread of conscious control snapped and I either gave up attempting to drive the vehicle or had the steering pulled away from me before the collision could take place. I blacked out, or at least have almost no memory of what came next.

Upon climbing the same route a month later, I realised that I was one small move away from an enormous 'thank goodness' hold. But in my emergency state, I knew only what had gone before me and I assume it must have taken some 30 seconds, or more, to reverse what I had climbed before arriving back to the safety of the easier, vertical wall.

I found myself coming around to still-screaming arms, but now my bodyweight was placed firmly on my feet. To my right was an escape route across enormous holds. I scurried like a rat abandoning ship and a minute later found myself on top of the cliff, staring at the brightest, most beautiful, sky I had ever seen. A small flock of cockatiels flew low over me and I experienced a state of profound gratitude for everything around me.

It was a moment I described afterwards as 'mystical', though, rather neglectfully, I never once apologised or thanked my unconscious for ignoring all of the signals it had sent, or for ultimately saving the show.

During my years as a full-time climber, this was just one experience of many that delivered a clear appreciation that our conscious mind, while an essential part of the team in most contexts, can also – at times – be more hindrance than help. In this example, I had experienced a growing discomfort in which my unconscious mind had clearly sent forth signals that I was unprepared for the task. Those signals continued and became stronger even as I pig-headedly, meaning consciously, pushed forward to achieve my goal. In the end, the only way to overrule any more stupid decisions by my conscious mind was for my unconscious to apparently take over and relieve my conscious mind with what I experienced as a blackout.

Had I been in better physical condition and not so jet-lagged, it would have been more likely that the signals I was aware of would have been far more supportive, even in the form of excitement and joy at such a task.

I am willing to speculate that you have similarly structured experiences in your life, even if you are not a climber or extreme-sports practitioner.

In a multitude of 'normal' events, our conscious awareness is shunted aside so that the unconscious mind can take over and provide the necessary degree of competence for the task at hand. How else would the reckless be able to drive at speed while listening to music, talking on their hands-free phone, and navigating all at the same time as slurping a drink (a common scene on my home highways of Los Angeles)? Even the grace of the elegant dancer depends on his/her release to unconscious processes, as does riding a bike, walking and a host of other unconscious competencies that we are each masters of. Think of any activity in which you are competent and then consider how little you have to consciously think about what you are doing. In most cases, there is almost no conscious thought at all. Each of us experiences unconscious competence in our lives, because if we didn't we'd have to consciously think about the endless small actions required for living. These include the very basics such as walking, moving our limbs to perform every task imaginable, forming words and body gestures to communicate and pretty much every action we take throughout a day without having to think consciously about how to do it.

Watch those same actions performed by a baby, or a person entirely new to a task such as driving, and you will see unconscious incompetence, until the action has been thoroughly learned.

Are you receiving?

When we begin to pay more attention to the signals that we experience throughout the day, it becomes apparent that our unconscious is always communicating with us in some form. For example, have you ever packed your things ready to walk out the door and begun to experience a vague feeling of resistance, or a sense of having forgotten something? As you often find out later, it would have been best to stop and scan the room, to give time for those sensations to guide your attention to a forgotten item, such as a phone or wallet.

We each experience communication from our unconscious, be it sensing danger before it happens, having resistance towards someone's alleged intentions or simply responding to a need for a walk and some fresh air.

The conscious mind is a little bit like the screen of a computer with the main operating system working out of sight and popping up information for consideration every few nanoseconds. The experience of our thinking in which we might be tempted to assume is 'the real us' is also the source of certain features such as deliberateness, solution-seeking, being attentive to information, being sequential, logical, linear and outcome-oriented, including a raft of organisational skills essential to success in the modern world. The conscious mind is superb at allocating solutions and goals and preferences to a multitude of contexts, such as, 'It will be good if I stop creating more debt on my credit cards', 'I'm not drinking alcohol for a month', 'I really don't need to eat dessert', 'I will never scream at my kids ever again', 'I'm going to write a book/start a project', 'I won't feel sick when the elevator doors close', 'I really am as good as she is', 'I won't shake and stutter this time when I make a speech'.

Unfortunately, without the unconscious being aligned with such conscious decision-making, we all know only too well how these types of command objectives can end when there is a mismatch in the person making the statement.

Long before the early days of Freudian psychiatry, we knew about our mythical hidden self, the unconscious. We often suspected it of an unpleasant set of qualities and it regularly received the blame for our behaviours that are primal, selfish, prejudiced, reactive, lazy – which we would rather not take responsibility for. But, really, what we are pointing our fingers at is the main event of human existence, wherein below our conscious awareness the majority of life-supporting processes occur. Consider how our grouping of living cells is managed by some yet unknown inner wisdom of biological orchestration. Our digestion, healing, immunity, vision, hearing, balance, energy production, detoxification, weight gain/loss, growth, reproduction, generation of speech are all performed without any conscious interference. In my opinion, it is time we stopped giving the unconscious such a hard time and appreciated it for all that it is, or rather, all that we are.

You're more than you think you are

The unconscious seems to exist in the realm of associations – good and bad; it (you and I) experiences feelings, altered states, makes intuitive judgements, seeks experiential learning (seemingly) and is predominantly non-verbal in its expression. Possibly, most important of all, is that our behaviours are mostly accessed from this system of form and energy, meaning that when we engage in productive, positive behaviours, without thinking about it, the unconscious is the source, as it is for behaviours of the opposite variety.

Yet, the difference between these two forms or types of processing – conscious and unconscious mind – seems to be absolutely distinct in their logic at least. What I mean by this is that we experience each version of our mind so differently that there is no overlap or confusion in how they operate. An example is communication and how words are used as a conscious expression of our experiences, whereas unconsciously we express through our body language, voice tone and timbre.

This experience in difference between the two minds, can, and has, led many of us to live with a combination of seemingly opposing parts that cause us to want one way of living while acting out another altogether. For those who manage to achieve alignment, the creation is a harmonious coordination that rallies towards the same dreams, goals and daily activities as one combined team.

Nothing could be harder than inhabiting the life of your dreams when the conscious and unconscious minds are at odds. You have likely had the experience where you seem to struggle and require excess effort to achieve certain outcomes. Maybe, like the mother who goes back to work for her career but spends all day pining for her child. Or the person who goes on a strict diet in order to look a certain way, when looking thin doesn't match up to the joy he or she experiences when eating great food with friends. I have worked with a number of utterly miserable, but financially successful, men and women who consciously chose to live their prime years in jobs that focus only on money and that they hated. Many of them felt a regular urge to be working in completely different types of 'fantasy' roles such as the arts, teaching, acting or being a fire-woman or pilot.

We can override our unconscious desires with pure determination, but will rarely escape from the feelings that tell us that we are out of alignment with our unconscious selves.

A question, then, is how can we bridge the gap between our conscious and unconscious mind and what does such an alliance look like? Let me offer a story that contains an example of what it's like when our two minds are not aligned.

A holy un-alliance

My new client had been smiling since the moment we met. I sat in his office, now in private, and he still smiled some 10 minutes after I had been introduced by one of the thousand or so assistants, who revered him. He spoke,

> **Swami:** 'The thing is, Mike, I have the perfect life here and it just doesn't make any sense.'
>
> **Mike:** 'Perfect? How, specifically, is it perfect?'
>
> **Swami:** 'I am supported by people who love me. I have all of my needs met – good food, beautiful surroundings, I travel business class around the world to many incredible destinations, I have assistants for any chores, I can read and study as much as I desire; we even have a black American Express card we can use for anything we might need.'

This last point was made with an even wider smile, for emphasis, but also an elevation in tone of voice that resembled a subtle, strangled squeal.

> **Mike:** 'So what don't you have?' I asked provocatively.
>
> **Swami:** 'What do you mean?'

Mike: 'I mean that no life is perfect, and there must be some things that you don't have access to?'

Swami: 'Not really. My guru is happy for me to privately read certain books, like right now, I am on the *Harry Potter* stories. We have use of the Internet and can experience life outside of the temple.'

Mike: 'You mean you can view how other people experience life outside of the temple? I'd hardly say that the Internet is a platform for direct experience of anything other than words and pictures. And it's obvious to me that you are extremely intelligent in some ways ... '

He nodded at the half-compliment.
I continued:

Mike: 'So how do all these rather, uh ... [I attempted a rare politeness] antiquated beliefs sit with you? You're telling me that all the women have to sit at the back of the room when you present so that they are as far away from you as possible? Doesn't that strike you as being sexist in a major way?'

Swami: 'No, no, no, you don't understand, Mike, they prefer it that way.'

This statement came with so much tension in his smile that I half expected his face to crack or nose to grow a few inches.

Mike: 'How do you know?' I challenged. 'You don't talk to them, so how do you know?'

Swami: 'Our teams speak with them.'

Mike: 'Yes, and your teams are made up of men who control what goes on in this organisation. It sounds like a load of sexist bullshit to me. A throwback from some era when female expression was repressed so that men could rule the block until their testosterone dried up and they needed their hair stroked. I get that if you're meant to be focusing on your spiritual life, whatever that means, that you don't need the sexual distractions, but say it for what it is, not some vaguely veiled lie that "they prefer it that way".'

Swami: 'No one has ever spoken to me like this, Mike,' he said with a look of intrigue on his face. 'I appreciate your honesty.'

Mike: 'Have you ever had sex?' I asked flatly.

Swami: 'No, of course not.'

Mike: 'Dude, you are missing out on something there,' I laughed.

Swami: 'I would be lying if I told you that I don't think about it.'

Mike: 'Uh, yeah, you know that psychologists estimate that men have 60,000 thoughts a day. Three are about food, a few hundred about football and the remaining 59,000 are all about sex!'

He laughed without any tension for the first time in our conversation.

I decided to provoke further with a fantasy offer.

Mike: 'Look, here's the plan. I'll come back tonight under the cover of darkness. You'll meet me at the back gate of the temple. I'll drive you into Soho, where we'll eat oysters and steak, drink fine red wine – on your black Amex – and then drink whiskey and smoke cigars at my favourite club. I'll get you back here before breakfast, stinking of smoke, alcohol and perfume. Deal?'

He squealed again, only this time in delight.

Swami: 'Deal, deal' he said in mock acceptance.

After we had finished laughing and imagining scenarios of his first taste of alcohol in a Soho bar, we turned to the reason he had called me.

Swami: 'I have pains all over my body, headaches, I wake lots at night and need the bathroom. We have extremely good doctors and medical support for all of the Swamis, but no one can find any cause for my symptoms.'

Mike: 'How long have you been a Swami monk?'

Swami: 'Twenty-two years, since I was 16 years old.'

Mike: 'When did the pain start?'

Swami: 'Maybe a year and a half ago.'

Mike: 'When did you start having reservations about your
monk life?'

This question was a total mind-read on my part, if what
Swami had said to me was to be accepted as true. However,
over the course of our conversation, I noted dozens of incon-
gruities in his physiology, or body language, when he justified
or defended the rather odd traditions he was trained in. When
he had informed me that touching cash, even accidentally,
came with the consequence of having to wash his hands 100
times, I asked, 'Why not 101, or 99?' When he had told me
that he would have to fast for 24 hours for standing on a
carpet that also had a woman standing on it, regardless of the
distance between them, I asked, 'What kind of female infec-
tion could be so rapidly spreading through carpet fibres?' I
also asked him if he was certain that no women had made
the orange gown he was wearing? In all of Swami's responses
I observed and heard a divide, or incongruence, between the
words with which he answered and the unconscious communication that he was unaware of. It was as if a logical, intelligent
man had swallowed a tape recorder and the playback loop was
on repeat for a series of entirely outdated and illogical beliefs.

I viewed Swami's symptoms as signals from his unconscious.
His symptoms were my leverage on him. If the life he was
living was so ideal and holy, why was he physically reacting to
his environment in such a way?

Swami: 'I guess we all have doubts at times.'

Mike: 'Some more than others?'

Swami: 'What else would I do?' He asked this while unconsciously
looking around his room to ensure that no one heard the
half-confession.

I waited for many long seconds so that he could ponder his
own question. I broke the silence.

Mike: 'What will you do?'

Where's the bridge?

Communication from our unconscious comes, for many of us, most clearly in the form of feelings and is an essential component of our state. You can validate this from direct experience, otherwise how would you know when to eat and replenish bottomed-out glucose levels? Without an appreciation for unconscious communication, you would likely stay awake until you collapsed as you ignored the signals for sleep. Going to the bathroom would be a hit-and-miss affair if you could not feel the sensations that tell you to empty your bladder. Similarly, though perhaps not so clear to many, is the feeling of drudgery or dread that arises on Sunday night or Monday morning before going back to work in a job you loathe and that has little value to you other than the illusion of security.

Our unconscious communicates to us constantly. For example, I am presently feeling a prod of urgency as I work on this book to a looming deadline that I will struggle to meet. I was woken at 05.45 (no alarm needed) this morning with a clear image of this chapter's remaining content. I considered going back to sleep for 20 minutes and then realised that my nervous system was fired up and ready. So I made the unusual gesture (to some) of thanking my unconscious, before tiptoeing out of bed, and using the energy that was mobilised for writing 1,000 words before my son woke and requested that I made him breakfast.

It often seems that communication between our two types of consciousness is a one-way channel, and that consciously we have little effect on what goes on in our unconscious. However, to become fluent in communication with our unconscious requires that we pay attention to its many and varied offers of wisdom that are delivered to us in the form of feelings, intuition, motivation, procrastination, creativity, fears, dreams and a wide range of accompanying images and sounds sometimes detected consciously, sometimes not, but all components of our 'state'.

The communication I am suggesting is not a language but a range of sensory experiences that many of us have switched off on the assumption that they are not as valid and real as what we might assume conscious, analytical, logical and organised thinking to be. In Western culture, at least, priority is given to the conscious mind over the unconscious, which is like driving a car and never considering all the moving parts that exist inside, below the surface coverings.

I have worked with many people who are extremely successful in very left-brain, conscious activities, such as working in engineering, science and tech, but who have lousy emotional lives or health because they ignore all messages that arise from their least-preferred aspect of consciousness. But it is important to know that it is all 'you' who is making your heart beat, 'you' who is managing those billions of cellular reactions, 'you' who is capturing vast realms of information, 'you' who is responsible for rare moments of genius, 'you' who is responsible for excessive moments of stupidity, 'you' are all of your processes, 'you' are your unconscious and it is 'you'. Which, in my experience, is cause for celebration, in that all of the potentially infinite resources that the unconscious is capable of providing, are *you*, to be accessed and utilised when aligned effectively with your conscious thoughts and desires.

To bring our two minds together in a working harmony, we can use a pattern that enables communication at both levels of mind. The steps below will enable both your conscious and unconscious mind to communicate between each other. I highly recommend using the videos or audio on the app and website.

PATTERN:

Unconscious signals

1. Find a comfortable spot to sit, away from any distractions.
2. Begin to self-calibrate to your current state by running the attention scanner (Chapter 1, see page 24) up and down your body and releasing any tense areas in your musculature.
3. Breathe in to a set count of three seconds. Hold for three seconds. Breathe out for three seconds. Hold for three seconds. Repeat this pattern for a couple of minutes.

Once you have accessed a relaxed state, you will begin by simply asking your unconscious mind to communicate with you directly by providing an involuntary signal of some kind, meaning that the signal does not arise consciously and that you cannot make it happen at will. The signal we are aiming for will naturally arise without your conscious effort.

1. In a relaxed state, ask internally: 'Unconscious mind, I propose that we communicate directly, if this is acceptable to you. Please provide me with a signal that means "yes".'
2. Now pay very close attention (more self-calibration) to any shifts in your experience of what you see, hear or feel.
3. If you are unaware of any signal, ensure you are suitably relaxed and request a signal: 'Unconscious mind, please communicate with me now by providing a signal for "yes".'
4. When you experience an involuntary sensation of some kind, such as muscular movement, feeling, sound or change in vision, it is important to test that it is involuntary by testing to ensure you cannot recreate the same signal with your conscious intent. For example, say your finger moves in a certain way or you feel a sensation in your chest. Can you consciously repeat the same movement or sensation? If you can, this is not a true unconscious signal and you can repeat your request. If you cannot make the sensation happen again consciously, you have a verifiable 'yes' signal.

5. When you are satisfied that you have an involuntary signal, ask your unconscious to amplify it: 'Unconscious, please amplify the strength of this signal if it is a "yes".'

6. Upon receiving confirmation, thank your unconscious for its cooperation with your conscious mind.

7. Repeat the same steps for a 'no' signal.

8. Now ask, 'Unconscious, please provide a signal for "no".'

9. Once you have a signal for 'no', test that it is involuntary by attempting to make it happen upon your conscious command.

As an example of my own unconscious signals, when I run this pattern, I usually experience a strong movement of my left calf muscles for 'yes' and small twinges in my face for 'no'. I am unable to duplicate these sensations upon request and regularly use them for direct communication between my unconscious and conscious mind, to align them and help me achieve what I want.

By align, I mean that I ask my unconscious to support me as an ally in gaining what I consciously desire, as well as taking responsibility for changing the behaviours that don't serve me at the conscious level.

Once you have verified that you have a genuine, involuntary signal from your unconscious, you are ready to make the most of your own neurology by asking the following questions.

PATTERN:

Creating an ally

1. 'Unconscious, is there any behaviour that you want to change that currently exists outside of my conscious awareness?' ('yes'/'no') If 'yes' ...

2. 'Will you ensure that these changes are ecological, meaning that when they happen they do so with positive effect in all areas of my life?' ('yes'/'no') If 'yes' ...

3. 'Unconscious, do you have the resources to make this change?' ('yes'/'no') If 'yes' …
4. 'Can you organise these resources to make the appropriate changes now?' ('yes'/'no') If 'yes' …
5. 'Can you complete these changes immediately or within X [you can request multiple periods, such as an hour, day, two days, week, etc] time frame?' ('yes'/'no') If 'yes' …
6. 'Will you start now?' ('yes'/'no')

If your unconscious replies with a 'no', you can ask:

1. 'Unconscious, is there a positive intention for "no"? And can you achieve this positive intention in some other way?'
or
2. You can extend the time frame.
3. You can change the way you ask your unconscious.

It is hard to know what to predict or expect when using this pattern. Unlike most coaching methods that consciously swap one type of behaviour for another, for example, swapping 'being hesitant' for 'being assertive', this pattern hands over all of the responsibility to the unconscious, which if you think about it, makes total sense, because almost all of our undesirable behaviours arise unconsciously, and attempting to change them through willpower, conscious understanding, or direct conscious command is not only hit and miss, it is like a very small tail trying to wag a very large dog.

I have used this pattern with people from all walks of life and despite it often seeming too simple, the effects are often dramatic and immediate.

Some people find that it can take more time and commitment to experience a signal from the unconscious, especially if the individual has spent a lifetime ignoring their unconscious communication, for a preferred form of left-brain, very logical and conscious, thinking.

A number of very analytical people can often have no obvious connection with their unconscious, and when this happens we use a different pattern to the same effect.

PATTERN:

The Sway signal (or human pendulum)

Note: It can be useful to have a person standing next to you to prevent you moving or falling too suddenly.

1. Stand with your legs together, eyes closed, head tilted back and knees locked straight.
2. Close your eyes and ask, 'Unconscious, please sway me in a pattern that I can take to mean "yes". '
3. Without consciously moving, pay attention to the involuntary direction of the sway.
4. Open your eyes and test this sway by repeating it consciously and noting if there is a difference in the quality of the sway when you repeat it intentionally.
5. Close your eyes and ask, 'Unconscious, please provide a pattern of sway by moving me in a direction that I can take to mean "no".' Pay attention to the sway.
6. Open your eyes and test this sway by repeating it consciously, noting if there is a difference in the quality of the sway when you repeat it intentionally.
7. When you are satisfied that your sway is involuntary, you can test by asking a number of simple 'yes'/'no' answer questions, such as 'Am I currently wearing a red sweater', etc.
8. You can now use this sway pattern to align with your unconscious and follow the earlier steps for creating an ally.

If you are unable to get a clear sway signal, you can ask, 'Unconscious, I propose that we communicate through an involuntary movement that means "yes". Is this acceptable to you?'

Forming an alignment with our unconscious is important for just about everything we do. One level communicates with precise (sometimes) words while the other communicates with feelings, symptoms and ideas. When we align the two we have powerful and effective access to more resources than when we operate predominantly in one level of mind over the other.

A right state of affairs

In Western culture, we give a lot of importance to the common sensations we call 'emotions', which are the involuntary or semi-involuntary states that we experience in different contexts. Many emotions affect people's lives in unwanted ways, be it raging in anger at the smallest of mistakes, getting embarrassed when speaking to strangers or suffering from the lows of regular depression. These sensations can, and do, rule the day-to-day lives of many people. Maybe if, alongside traditional subjects such as maths and science, we also taught kids from the earliest ages how to change and choose their states, we might have a considerably healthier world.

Unfortunately, some of the official guardians of emotions tend to be those within therapeutic systems who inform us that bringing our unwanted feelings to the surface is the key to happiness and becoming a better person. I've personally experienced anger therapy that was deemed to be essential for ridding people of repressed guilt, shame, hatred and negative emotions that needed to 'come out'. I also know of many clients who have been consciously guided into releasing repressed anger, by accessing a memory they believed to be the cause of their unwanted states. This 'repression of feelings' is often assumed to be responsible for an individual's lack of emotional stability, and can be used as a justification for all manner of un-useful behaviours. For example, 'I did it because of my repressed guilt/anger/shame, etc, therefore it was not "me" at all.'

Metaphors can be life-changing in both good and bad ways and the metaphor of 'repressed' when used alongside emotions is one that I would heavily warn against accepting.

The 'repressed' label may have been a useful description a hundred years ago when we knew less about neurology and psychology, but descriptions need updating to keep pace with current knowledge. Repressed and pushed-down emotions actually do not exist in the way they are generally presented. How could they? The term is referring to billions of electrical signals that are experienced in our neurology. If you push them down, are they being squashed into your legs?

By accepting that these sensations happen to us for no reason, be they 'anger', 'sadness', 'depression' or 'happiness', 'triumph', 'confidence', we tend to reinforce victim identity, 'it just happens to me' and the belief that these states are in some way independent from us, rather than being a) messengers and b) within our ability to change and choose as we learn from the experiences.

Does anyone in our modern world still believe that the arrow of 'Cupid' causes the feeling of love? If not, then why do we accept that emotions are like shots from some deep space inside our system?

I am not saying we should become like robots and avoid experiencing a range of emotions, but rather that it is important to always have the choice to experience them or not. There may well be times and places when anger, sadness, shyness, and the like, are appropriate or useful, and there are also times when we're better off changing to a more useful and resourceful state of some kind. Having the choice over our states makes a life-changing difference to everything we do.

But wait ... is this not contradictory to my suggestion that we each bring more attention to the signals that arise from our unconscious?

Yes, it is and ... there is a balance, by allowing our unconscious prompts and intuition to guide us, combined with the ability to change any unpleasant states once the message has been received and acted upon.

A good friend of mine is a great example. Bella was once asked to give a last-minute talk to a large group of people, but with less than an hour of preparation time. She is known as a great speaker and she loves presenting. What is not known about her is that she plans her talk material meticulously, right down to the pauses. On this occasion, she had never given a last-minute presentation in her life and when asked to do so, she experienced a very unpleasant sensation of anxiety in her belly and throat. She knew this was her unconscious way of making known the deep aversion she has to being unprepared for anything. In her words, 'I'm a happy control freak who likes to have a hold of the reins.'

Bella acknowledged the unpleasant state that arose from her agreement to give the impromptu talk and then decided that if she were going to present, she would need to be in a more resourceful, even optimum, state. So she walked around a lot and shifted her breathing and physiology with some of the methods she had learned in one of my workshops. For once, she gave almost no consideration to what she was going to talk about and trusted that she knew enough already. With only minutes to go, her only focus was what state she would be in when she stepped on stage. Bella spoke freely and creatively about her subject for 45 minutes. When she finished, she knew that it was not anywhere near her usual standard of detailed thoroughness, but she both enjoyed it more than any presentation before, and she received great feedback from the event promoters.

What intrigued me most was the epiphany Bella received from the event. On the way home, as she pondered her new state of jubilation and freedom, she created a new interpretation for her earlier unpleasant feelings prior to presenting. She now viewed her nerves and discomfort not as a sign to be more prepared, but as a sign that she needed to loosen up, become more flexible and be more willing to take a few risks in all areas of her life.

Choose your labels

As a 20-second experiment, choose an emotion that you commonly experience and change its name to 'a sequence of electrical impulses being experienced by my neurology'.

If you are someone who has labelled yourself with an emotional identity, such as 'I'm a very jealous person', what happens when you change the language you use to describe your state? Try changing it to, for example, 'I'm a system of nerves that experiences a lot of electrical charges in different contexts' or, 'I get so electrically charged in my neurology when certain triggers set the sequence of neuronal pathways off.'

If you regularly declare that 'I get angry' or 'I am overcome with sadness', or 'I'm green with envy', you have accepted in some way that these states are happening to you and that you have little or no choice over their effect on your life.

That is not to say that we do not each have a range of learned emotional responses and behaviours from when our mirror neurons were at their most active. The human unconscious can, in a very crude way, be compared to a vast super-computer or storage vault containing endless units of experience that clearly pop up as reactions and which none of us is likely to ever delete the memory of. Not that I would want to delete any of them, either. For even the most traumatic events of our past can become important lessons once we can access them without suffering unwanted reactions. Having choice over which states we access and associate to which memories or present contexts, is something of a fantasy for many people, even though most of us naturally choose and change our states when the situation provokes it anyway.

In my form of coaching work I mostly expose my clients to the contexts in which their unwanted states are experienced.

As the client begins to start his or her slide into the unwanted state, I then interrupt it in some way so that the sequence of those connections between neurons is broken. This reliably has the effect of creating new connections that display different responses, as the following story will highlight.

Cool it

Roy was a 30-something businessman whose relationship was near to failing because of his uncontrollable outbursts of anger. In a last-ditch effort to get some help, his partner had sent Roy my way. When he arrived to my office, he was limping a little. I knew the story already but asked because I suspected I could use it to provoke his anger.

> **Mike:** 'What's up with your limp?'
> **Roy:** 'I got upset about something and kicked a cast-iron bed. I've badly bruised my toe.'
> **Mike:** 'You're an idiot,' I replied flatly.

I then asked him to remove his shoes in my polished wooden-floored office. He did so hesitantly.

> **Mike:** 'So,' I asked gruffly, while reaching to take his shoes. 'What the hell are you doing here?'

He passed me his brogues and I flung them roughly towards my own shoes, which were neatly placed in the corner of the room.

> **Roy:** 'Ellie [his partner] told me I had to come see you, or else.'
> **Mike:** 'Personally, I think she's stupid to allow your relationship to last this long,' I muttered
> **Roy:** 'F*ck you,' he replied with a sudden reddening of his face.
> **Mike:** (Nonchalantly) 'Do you want a glass of water?'
> **Roy:** 'Sure.'

I went to my office kitchenette and poured a large glass of water. As I brought it back, I feigned a missed footing and stepped firmly on his bruised foot. This was the trigger for what I was aiming to provoke in Roy.

He exploded:

Roy: 'Ow! You idiot! What the hell are you doing?'

I immediately threw the whole glass of water over him, ignoring his response entirely as I casually sat back down on my chair.

Roy stared at me incredulously, shocked that his work suit was now soaked while I was half-smiling, half-cocking an eye, as if to say, 'What's the problem?' After five seconds, he began to chuckle.

Roy: 'Do you have a towel?'
Mike: 'Nah – relax and cool off, the water will help.'

He laughed again.

Roy: 'I don't get it.'
Mike: 'I was told you were being controlled by your anger and that you get lost in these rages. It seems to me that you can cool off pretty easily. Just tell Ellie to carry a large glass of water around wherever you go. Maybe you can learn to wear your states as you do your clothes, so you can change both as easily as each other.'

Over the years, my work has connected me with teenagers and adults who have been subjected to horrific forms of abuse and even, in one case, many days of torture by troops. To suggest that such experiences can be in our neurology without them having an impact upon the emotional states of the affected may seem disrespectful and insensitive. But my position is that I can still have a deep respect for a person and what they have been through while simultaneously being disrespectful and contemptuous towards the states and behaviours they experience when they are being affected negatively.

Next time you find yourself in a context where your unconscious presents you with an unwanted state, ask yourself the following question: Is it preferable to accept it and hope it goes away before you make some regrettable actions, or to be lightning-fast at recognising the onset of the sensations and then able to interrupt it before it can take effect?

I am certain as to what my own preference is, and will shift my physiology, breathing and perception (by stepping into Third Position, see page 42), the moment I sense the first signals leading to an unwanted state of any kind.

How we do it

When you look at the many everyday examples of people's actions, it becomes apparent that (unless we consciously interrupt the pattern) our behaviours are influenced by our states, and our states are influenced by the contexts we find ourselves in.

I feel relatively safe in saying that it is unlikely you will trigger the same states at, say, an airline check-in desk when you are told it is too late to check in, compared to lying on a beach and enjoying an accompanying cocktail (though the choice to feel whatever you like in both cases is always available to you).

Even as you read this book and consider those two different contexts, you may be able to discern the difference in sensations that arises from simply thinking about them.

I invite you now to choose a context in which you would usually have an unpleasant experience and think about it for 20 seconds ...

Now give your body a little shake to clear the feeling and think instead of a really pleasant context. As you do this, hallucinate the sights as if you are seeing directly through your own eyes, and hearing through your ears. If you have connected to the sights and sounds clearly in this exercise, you will notice a difference in bodily sensations and feelings.

In many cases, it matters little if we are directly experiencing an event or simply thinking about it. Be they real or hallucinated, sounds and images trigger a sequence of reactions inside us that we experience as our state.

When I am away from home and I think of cuddling my kids, I get into an instant state of warmth and love. If I am careless enough to think about bad news, or the condition of the world's poorest people, I can easily find myself having unwanted feelings and thoughts.

A really common example of how hallucinations can affect us is when people worry. Worry, by its structure, is the predicting of future events with a negative outcome. We don't worry about something that is actually taking place, and it often takes an exhausting toll on us if we worry about events for too long.

But worry, like any prompt from the unconscious, can be used as a really useful signal to take action and get underway on some plan that might prevent the worrying event from ever fully happening.

I have coached a small number of people who were worried about the debt they had accumulated. Once they learned how to change the unpleasant states they were experiencing, I then asked them to write a budget for their monthly income and expenses. In all three people, there was an obvious shift after only 10 minutes of working out where they could save money (on often trivial and unnecessary things and activities) in order to begin paying off their debts.

But what if you find yourself worrying about events you have little control over, such as an asteroid collision? I admit that I personally know of no strategy to avert such an event and, in this case, as with all stressful events, simply shifting the unpleasant state to a new one of your choosing seems the most obvious choice.

Conjuring up negative images is often all that is required to trigger an unpleasant rush of stress hormones. Indeed, more often than not what we conjure up internally in the way of pictures and sounds is often far worse than any version of real life that we may have to respond to. By picturing and/or hearing a bad event, person or news, we get to experience all of the accompanying sensations that go along with it.

This happens to all of us regularly, in both positive and negative ways. The term 'synaesthesia' is used to describe when a sensory input (such as a sound, touch, taste, smell, sight) in one part of our system stimulates an experience, such as physical feeling/state, in another sensory channel. Sight triggers images, sounds trigger hearing, touch triggers feeling and so on. Without synaesthesia we would be unlikely to feel the deep joy of seeing our loved ones happy. Food might taste good but have no satisfying effect on our hunger. Music would have little effect on inspiring us to tap our feet or dance.

Do you remember:

- The **warmth** of **sound** when you and your partner used to sing together?
- The **smell** of those foods that you **loved** as a child?
- The **image** you recall of your first **excited** day at school or work?
- The **sight** of the face of someone who **intimidates** you?
- The **taste** of the alcohol, after which you **felt** sick for days?

Our capacity to experience in multiple sensory channels provides a deep, flavoursome, colourful, gushing richness in our internal world, all blended into one experience that our nervous system generates at any one time.

Synaesthesia also holds the key to freeing ourselves from anxiety, fear, doubt, shame, anger, stress, embarrassment and any other states we might wish to experience less of, by connecting positive states to what we deem to be unpleasant sights and sounds.

Act as if

For the majority of people, states are experienced as involuntary, but for some they are not. Actors are trained to access emotional states on cue, and can recognise the sequence of how their emotions are triggered, perhaps recalling an image first and then a shift in breath and physiology. If, like an actor, you were to be filmed as you shifted from one state to another (let us use one example of many options, say, 'relaxed' into 'excited') you could easily observe from looking back at your recording that a number of obvious 'surface' changes (corresponding to below the surface) take place in your body.

These likely include a change in musculature – perhaps your shoulders lift, your arms move with more speed and range of motion, your mouth and eyes expand their aperture, your spinal cord straightens and so on. If you slowed down the replay of your recording, it would likely reveal your breathing shifting dramatically, even before your muscular system had reacted. Maybe, as your state shifts, your lungs expand from low volume, upper-chest breathing, to high volume, full-belly expansion. This happens so fast that we are rarely aware that we have even shifted.

State changes can also be noted with our eyes closed, just as long as the person is speaking. As the breath and physiology change, so does the stream of air and sounds that come out, by which I mean speech. Listen with eyes closed to the beginning of any inexperienced public speaker and you will likely hear throat tension in the tone, timbre, pitch and pace of their words.

So if our breathing and physiology changes unconsciously (involuntarily) in the process of shifting from one state to another, would it not make sense that by reversing the pattern and consciously manipulating our breathing and physiology, we can change how we feel, by choice?

This, in part, is how better actors call up real emotions on cue.

Some years ago, I signed up for a month of method-acting classes and noted how the noticeably great actors in the group were able to cry on command. Though I have no idea what the images and sounds were that they used as a stimulus when they cried, they all shifted (some more subtly than others) their breathing and physiology, making tiny adjustments of their facial muscles as they turned on the waterworks.

What surprised me was how few of the well-trained actors used these same skills to adjust and choose their emotions in everyday life. I have asked a number of actors what the difference between choosing their states in a controlled environment, such as a stage, as opposed to the theatre we call real life is? It had not occurred to anyone I spoke to that their same skills could be used in multiple contexts.

As a trainer and coach, I have the use of numerous methods to assist people with changing unwanted behaviours and, over the years, I have learned to avoid working with clients in a safe, cosy therapeutic environment, especially as the contexts in which they experience problems exist mostly in the outside world. Beyond the therapist's chair there may well not exist a world of understanding, wishing upon stars and fairy dust. And, unsurprisingly, the very contexts we most need to work in are most often the contexts we avoid at all costs.

You may assume that by staying clear of undesirable situations, you can remain free from their effects, but the problem is that when we experience unwanted states in one context, there is often an overlap to others. So it is almost always better to directly experience what we want to avoid most and then change our state as we do so.

PATTERN:

State transfer

1. From Third Position, choose a context in your life in which you want to experience a more positive state and behaviour.

2. In a physical location 'A', hallucinate yourself in that chosen context, seeing yourself experiencing the unwanted state and behaviour that commonly accompanies it, and step into the physical location so that you are in the context, looking through your own eyes.
3. Notice the undesirable state while in the context.
4. Step out and spend 10 seconds shaking and moving your body to break the negative state.
5. Now recall* a time and place when you were at your best. See and hear yourself back in that context until you can feel the 'at your best' positive state developing. Adjust your physiology by straightening your spine and releasing any tension.
6. When you're satisfied that a positive state has been generated, step back into location 'A' and see and hear the elements of it.

Now step out again and repeat steps 1–5 until you can step into the chosen context, 'A', without experiencing any of the negative states that previously arose in it.

*If you have challenges recalling a time when you are at your best, you can ask 'What would I be doing and how would I feel if I was at my absolute best?' Use this question to generate the states that might come from the answer.

Fear of flying

Roger worked for a large corporation that required him to travel a lot. Within minutes of taking off on a standard flight from an airport in Mexico, the pilot informed the passengers that they were about to perform an emergency landing as one engine had cut out. The plane came in flapping like a shot bird and seconds before contact with the runway Roger saw the ground coming towards his window on his left side. He tensed up hard in anticipation for impact, but because of the skills of the pilot, impact never came.

Roger had developed such an intense fear of flying as a result of this experience that he was now sedating himself heavily in preparation for each work flight, with the consequence that he was useless for the few days he spent in each new country. His extreme fear was also now surfacing in other contexts and he found himself unable to give presentations without breaking out in sweats and hand tremors. His boss had given him two weeks' leave to seek therapy and sort out his problems. Roger had already received a number of cognitive behavioural therapy sessions and experienced no difference to his fear. Upon hearing his story, I asked what he was doing that Friday. His response:

Roger: 'Nothing, except trying to sort out my head.'

As luck would have it, I was making one of my regular visits to Mallorca that weekend. It was the perfect opportunity to get Roger into the context he most avoided.

Mike: 'Great, I don't have time to work with you in my office this week, but meet me at Gatwick on Friday and get yourself booked on the same flight as me to Mallorca.'

After a conversation that required me to convince Roger to lay off his sedatives before joining me, he agreed to fly and have his own short break in the sun. We met at the airport and discussed everything except his phobia. I was keen to work with Roger on the plane and to see when his nervous system started its sequence into the phobic state.

Roger: 'I have my pills, just in case', he admitted.

Roger was agitated from the moment we started boarding. We sat in seats next to each other and as the engines started up, he began to rub his hands as if they were cold. His skin colour changed along with his breathing. His body tensed at multiple points. I talked Roger through the relaxation and breathing exercise, guiding him to count his breaths and run a scan of his physiology.

He followed my instructions and began the deep breathing. I suggested that he went into peripheral vision so as to prevent recall of the plane-crash images he had been making over and over. He then relaxed his muscles in all the areas he could consciously identify tension. I was satisfied he was ready to fly. We took off and despite following the pattern of breath and tension release, Roger's hands began to shake, his skin drained of colour and sweat appeared on his brow. And yet I could see no tension in his jaw, shoulders, arms or breathing. I cracked a couple of jokes, to no effect. Then I realised that my seating position, on his right side, meant that I was unable to see his entire physiology. I leaned forward from my cramped position to get a full view of him. The missing piece of the puzzle appeared. His left shoulder was an inch or two higher than his right, and so tight and stuck in a position that looked like a bad impression of the hunchback of Notre Dame. By sitting on Roger's right side, I had missed the point in his physiology that was holding his fear in place.

I pressed his left shoulder down and began playing something I call 'the ripple game'. I push and the other person has to let the push ripple throughout their body with the least amount of muscular tension possible. The person being pushed is encouraged to be like jelly and aim not to resist the pushing but let it ripple through their very relaxed body. Within two minutes of him moving, jelly-like (and the person sitting next to him by the window getting a little unnerved), along with the breathing pattern, Roger was feeling his old relaxed self when in the air. He even laughed at more of my bad jokes. Landing was a breeze and two days later, on the return flight home, I sat many seats apart from him. Once in the air, I went to the bathroom to observe him casually. He smiled and confirmed with a thumbs-up that all was well, as it continues to be years later.

Roger, like many people, had assumed that he needed to 'sort his head out'. But when it comes to changing our states and behaviours, our head is only the top part of the whole person.

PATTERN:

Breathe and ripple

You can use the breathe-and-ripple combo in most contexts in which you experience unpleasant reactions. It's best to ask a friend or partner to accompany you and act as a guardian* or coach.

If you can't get a partner for this exercise, you can also use your imagination and see/feel as if you are being pushed at different locations in your body to respond with the ripple.

The first stage is to use the breath only. Add the body pushing as you enter the context.

1. From Third Position, identify a context that you usually avoid or experience an undesirable state in. We will name this context X.
2. Hallucinate context X in a physical location somewhere in the space that you currently inhabit.
3. Visit the context and associate to what you see and hear for long enough to experience the usual sensations that arise in the real-world version of this context. Stay here for ten seconds or until you have fully 'felt' the usual state that accompanies what you see and hear in this context. Leave the context and shake/move your body vigorously for ten seconds.
4. With your coach holding your arm to move it gently to the rhythm of your breath, begin the following breathing pattern (or a similar pattern that works for you to build a relaxed, alert state):

Three seconds inhale,
Three seconds hold,
Three seconds exhale,
Three seconds hold.

5. While continuing this breathing pattern, walk towards the hallucinated context X. If, at any point, you or your coach becomes aware of a falter in the breathing or excess tension in the arm, stop and re-set the breathing pattern again. The aim is to enter the context with the breathing pattern intact and without any tension in the body.

6. Once in the context, and retaining the breathing pattern, your coach can now push you just firmly enough to move you a little off-balance. Your role is to respond to the pushes by allowing your body to sway and move as if rippling like the surface of water, while continuing with the breathing.

An everyday application of this pattern is to identify real-world contexts that you desire to have a better experience within. Approach the contexts (in the real world) with a friend or coach and repeat the steps as you did for the hallu-cinated context. As an example, a person who gets anxious in crowded places would approach a real crowded place while breathing in a rhythm and being gently pushed/rippled.

*A guardian of state. The guardian/coach's role is to ensure the participant retains a breathing pattern that allows him or her to remain relaxed and alert.

CHAPTER 6

FREEDOM FROM FEARING MISTAKES

The degree to which we are willing to risk and push beyond our perceived capabilities will have a direct impact upon our successes. Mistakes, when viewed as learning experiences, are essential in our development.

'Experience is simply the name we give our mistakes.'

Oscar Wilde

Three in the morning can be an eerie time to run along mountain trails, especially when following a man wearing white robes, a strange hat and straw sandals, from which his toes hang over the front edge. Our guide around this natural assault course had yet to speak to us. Not a single word had been uttered and we had followed his lead since midnight. Most of our running and fast-walking for the previous three hours had been single file across trails that covered this mountain like a web. Without the ghostly figure who led us we would have been lost moments after starting our journey. Along the route, we passed dozens of car-sized mounds of earth at which the 'ghost' paused to give offerings of prayer and a small green leaf that looked like bay.

The distance we were to cover this night was somewhere in the region of 40 kilometres. Only one stop would be allowed for refreshments, at a temple, which, unbeknownst to us, was still two hours away. Our group of four consisted of a friend who ran triathlons, the monk who was our guide and my wife, who had requested a special grant from the head abbot to run with us, but respectfully behind us by at least 10 metres. To this day, my wife is likely to be the only woman in history to have travelled the trails of Japan's Mount Hiei with one of its legendary 'marathon monks'.

Our marathon monk was a devotee of the school of Tendai, a Buddhist practice that seeks enlightenment through ritual and meditation, which, in the case of the Hiei monks, is the ritual of running a marathon, or more, every single night for 100 days, just for starters.

Should a monk wish to commit to the big aim of enlightenment, he does so by running 1,000 nights in a row, stopping only after day 700 for a little sit-down, of sorts. The break in running is to allow for the 'Doiri', a process in which it is claimed that a monk must stay awake for nine days and nights and is not allowed to consume even a single mouthful of food or water. Plenty of monks have died during this extreme ascetic quest, possibly in preference to enduring yet another day of staying awake in a strict sitting position while dying of dehydration.

Our monk was on day 84 of his 100-night commitment. He had had his maximum allotted three hours' sleep the evening before, which had been preceded by a day of chores, meditation and chanting.

Hiei is a truly wild and beautiful place. Untouched forests shroud a number of 1,000-year-old temples, which give the impression of crouching when viewed in relationship to the ancient trees that cover Japan's holiest mountainside. I had run the previous night for TV cameras, the inclusion of which interrupted my attempts at any Zen-like concentration and an appreciation for the gift of this opportunity. I had requested to run again a second night to experience the mountain and ritual behaviour of a Tendai trainee fully, which was something of a unique lesson in discipline and dedication.

After five hours of totally silent fast-walking and jogging, we arrived at a group of small temples at the base of the mountain.

We followed the monk to the outer arch of the smallest building. He beckoned us all to sit, though without making eye contact with my wife. After disappearing behind a door for a minute, he returned with snacks and hot tea for all of us. We thanked him in our awful Japanese.

Monk: 'I speak a little English.'

Mike: 'Oh, wow, we didn't know and we were told not to speak to you.'

Monk: 'It is okay to speak here. We are resting.'

We ate our food and made some smalltalk about his previous life in an office in Tokyo.

Mike: 'Can I ask you a question?'

Monk: 'Please?'

Mike: 'Why do you carry a knife?'

Monk: 'We each carry a knife and a rope to remind us that we must not fail.'

Mike: 'I don't understand?'

Monk: 'It is tradition that if we fail or give up we should hang ourselves from a tree or take our lives with a knife [he gestured a disembowelling motion]. This was the fate of the monks who we give offerings to around the mountain.'

Mike: 'The mounds are monks who took their own lives?'

Monk: 'Yes, all around the mountain.'

All three of us went silent at this realisation.

My friend Michael asked the question that was on all of our minds

Michael: 'Will you use the knife or the rope if you fail?'

There was another short and awkward silence before the monk looked at us and started laughing.

Monk: 'I won't use either. We do not kill ourselves for failure any more. That is an old tradition that we have stopped many years ago. None of us wants to fail, but …'

He paused.

Monk: 'It is human to do so.'

How do you define failure?

Just as it seems there can be no absolute meaning to life, there can be no absolute degree of success or failure carved for each of us in stone. I have been intrigued to hear from a multi-millionaire client who still regularly works late into the night as he attempts to achieve his own idea of financial freedom. I also have two friends who retired in their fifties after selling their house and buying a tiny yacht to live out the rest of their lives in South America on less retirement money than it costs to buy a new family car. In their words, they are finally living their dream.

We all decide, from our own values, what failure and success mean to us personally. Both are learned concepts that we accept and adopt in the same way as concepts of good/bad, beautiful/ugly.

One man's meat is another man's poison.

One man's freedom fighter is another man's terrorist.

One man's success is another's nightmare.

Our definitions of success and failure also change with time and context. Since having kids, my new measure of failure is set by the amounts of time I spend away from my family. Previously, it was gauged by how much time I spent hanging on rock faces in exotic destinations.

If you speak to any person who has survived a terminal illness, you will also get an updated version of what success and failure looks like to them.

You may set your own standards by a gold medal, making a million dollars with the click of a button, being promoted to CEO, winning awards or flying into space (this latter is a dream I am working towards). Such goals are certainly worthy in the form of our culturally judged symbols of success. But success by other people's definition rarely adds up. Especially as the people we may be tempted to gauge our success and failure by are basing their own definitions upon the values of those who went before them and those before them.

If there was no one to pat you on the back, cheer for you, pay you, write about you, gossip about you and you were doing what you do entirely for your own satisfaction and meaning; what would you do and how would you define your success? Use the space below to fill in your responses, or use your own notebook/journal.

Success to me is _____

And _____

And _____

The same need to define our own terms is useful when related to failure. If we accept definitions of success or failure outside of our own making, we are asking for trouble.

I often wonder how many bright young things have fizzled out because their families or teachers have already planted within them the worst-case scenarios of their dreams and put them off even trying.

Parent: 'You do realise that you have only a one-in-a-million chance of becoming a successful professional and that you're better off getting a solid job at a bank?'
Child: 'Why?'
Parent: 'Because becoming a number-one-selling pop star is unlikely, therefore anything less is failure.'

'Because doing what you love for ten years, though it means playing at weddings, pubs and parties isn't good enough. Such activities would barely cover your modest outgoings and will never buy you the right to own the debt of a mortgage, shiny car and other life trappings. It matters little that you will do what you love every day.'

If there was no one to put you down, boo at you, con you, criticise you, gossip about you and you were doing what you do entirely for your own satisfaction and meaning, what would you do and how would you define failure? Use the space below to fill in your responses, or your own notebook/journal.

Failure to me is _____

Success and failure will always be whatever definition we accept them to be and the clearer we are on what is important to us, the better. I know from clients how easy it is to fail in business when working only for the financial gains rather than the satisfaction of the work. In my own case some years ago, having walked away from a business I spent six years building, the result was actually a great success in terms of freeing up my time so that I could work doing what I most value.

In my younger years, some of the most satisfying days of my life were also when I was flat broke, living out of a rusty old van, being an educational, financial, social deadbeat disaster by the standards of many. However, I got to wake up when I wanted, climb in beautiful places every day, meet crazy road-tripping counter-culture folks and read all my favourite authors, including Henry David Thoreau, while living a little in the spirit of his words.

'Go confidently in the direction of your dreams! Live the life you've imagined.'

But what stops most of us from going confidently in the direction of our dreams?

Or rather, what stops you?

How often are you fearful of failure and making mistakes, despite there being only a small number of potential outcomes that we might experience as failure?

Commonly these are:

- Not wanting to look bad/stupid in the opinion of others.
- Being scared of losing or damaging a reputation.
- Risking physical pain or harm.
- Losing a job, likely preventing countless creative talents from shining bright.
- Risking money or assets that might be at risk should you get it wrong.

Exercise:

Make a list of your biggest desires, goals and dreams.

_____

_____

Which of the previously listed fears have you viewed as hurdles towards achieving those dreams?

These fears have validity, right? After all, no one wants to lose their house on a stock tip; their job on a careless presentation; old people might avoid exercise for fear of breaking a hip; no eatery desires to lose its reputation by inadvertently poisoning its customers through experimental cooking ...

Yes, and no.

Money and assets are always at risk, even while you sleep. Just ask any Cypriot. Most of the country's wealthy population had 30 per cent of their wealth removed recently by their government while they were sleeping one night. Russians have, out of nowhere, seen the value of the rouble drop through the floor in just days.

No reputation is etched in stone. For every person who respects your actions, others will have contempt. How could anyone ever satisfy the opinions of seven billion unique reality tunnels?

Fear of pain is fear of life. Living wrapped in cotton wool with your days spent sitting in a soft, comfortable chair, rarely venturing forth, will bring with it as serious a set of symptoms (or worse) than a person might risk while learning to trampoline at the age of 80. The human body was, and is, designed for constant movement and the more adept we are at moving, the more likely we are to avoid physical injury.

Your job is as safe as the economy that supports it and global recessions exist in the cycle of gain and loss that is inherent in a capitalist system. Just ask any of the recently laid-off folks at some of the world's most profitable companies, such as Microsoft.

Not so long ago one of the world's top three restaurants inadvertently poisoned hundreds of customers with 'norovirus', and yet, it is still impossible to get a table within three months of calling. Mass food poisoning is a pretty big mistake to make, but it didn't stop that restaurant from continuing to do what it does best.

It seems that far too many of us are concerned with what others might think, partly because of our own lack of awareness regarding who we are and what position we take on matters.

If you care about what other people think of you, you will be wasting a lot of energy. Your body type, hair colour, clothing choices, accent, street address, car, vocation, beliefs, preferences and almost every element of your life that is on public display is judged by others. Try controlling or concerning yourself with that mass of primitive sorting procedures and you will drive yourself insane.

Wanting to be liked, appreciated and respected seems to be relevant to most of us and there is often a lot of pleasure to be experienced from achieving positive opinions from others, certainly more so than being viewed negatively. However, freedom to be ourselves and create lives of our choosing comes when we can accept others' appreciation without being motivated by it in any way.

I will assume that when you get a positive opinion, you experience a positive state. Similarly, if someone criticises you, you likely experience an unpleasant or reactive state. A simple way to dissociate from such feedback is to use the perceptual positions that you learned in Chapter 2 (Freedom from living (only) in your head).

By stepping into Second Position and taking on the values and beliefs of the person providing the criticism, you may realise how wildly subjective such feedback from that person is. You could even attempt to Second Position every person who is critical of you and you will realise what an utterly futile pattern you are engaging in.

It is also highly useful to step into a Third (observer) Position. Adjust your breathing and physiology and then observe the critic and the receiver, that latter being yourself when in First Position.

From a genuine Third Position that is clean of any of your own First Position programming, you are likely to observe that both the critic and the receiver have such highly subjective opinions on what is valuable that the criticism is purely an outpouring of one narrow reality tunnel to another. It can be advantageous to take from the critic what may be useful as way of instruction in how to behave better, but only if that instruction has validity to your own values.

I once played a game with myself for a couple of days that I had originally intended to play for a week. Throughout the day I acted as if I was a specific type of person who was a long way from how I am in most of my life. I took on the role of a highly organised accountant, an authoritarian headmistress, a military commander, a priest, a born-again believer, an assassin, a staunch atheist, an unmotivated slob, a pharmaceutically driven psychiatrist (actually the most difficult for me) and a bunch of other roles I cannot even remember now. From those multiple Second Positions, I then critiqued the outward appearance of who Mike is from a range of his activities in work and home life.

The opinion I developed of Mike from all of these different positions was one that had almost no resemblance with the one that I held of myself. It was a great example of how concerning ourselves with the opinions of others is a zero sum game.

Saving for rainy days

Planning for the future holds a lot of important benefits. However some people live so far in a future in which they predict bad outcomes, that they never appreciate life in the now. But the future never arrives and so being afraid of living in this moment is to let the only time we have slip by, as so many people seem to do.

My friend Edith is in her eighties. I have known her since I was a small child. She told me stories when I was young about the many nights she sheltered in bunkers while air raids destroyed the homes and lives of her friends and neighbours. She grew up in tough times in a rough part of England, with 11 brothers and sisters in a three-bedroom house. As a kid, she ate meals mostly consisting of potato and home-laid eggs and told me of her delight when she was able to buy fruit once a month upon leaving home as a 17-year-old. Her own mother died an agonising death of cancer at only 54 years. Her father died shortly after.

Edi had six children, only two of whom are alive today. She lost twins a few short days after their birth, a boy who lived to be one month old and her older, first-born adult son, who died in an accident in his twenties. Edi's own brothers and sisters have fallen off their perches over the years. Of the 12 family members, she is one of five remaining. She worked in countless jobs, scrubbing kitchens, cooking, working on buses, as a nurse and later in care for the elderly.

She has a kidney disease, cancerous cells in her liver, osteoporosis, angina, heart disease, a non-working thyroid, loss of hearing, endless back and joint pains and diabetes. She has saved money all her life and has enough cash tucked away to go on a cruise for the next 20 years. Without exception, every time I drop by to see her she tells me she is bored, lonely and in need of adventure. I point out that she can afford to take off and enjoy her last years in the sunshine, sipping piña coladas with her toes in the sand. 'What stops you?' I ask. Her reply is usually the same: 'I don't want to spend my money on holidays in case I need it for a rainy day.'

But what if, like Edi, your rainy days never actually come because you deal with them as they arise in the process we call 'living'?

Risk aversion

I have divided some of my years between living in the UK and the USA. It is my experience that Americans are way more open to risk and failure than my fellow Brits. I have mentioned this in conversations with American friends and we have loosely concluded that 'tall poppy syndrome' (the cutting down of any person/child who dares poke their head above the median) is nowhere near as prevalent in American culture.

Some cultures are generally encouraged to be more modest and respectful of existing paradigms, rather than looking for ways to disrupt the present new modes of operation. Many of the tech folks I have met and worked with in California are obsessed with finding ways to turn the world on its head and break from all and any traditions, regardless of how much and badly they could fail while doing so. It is this form of attitude that is turning many such people into multi-millionaires and changing our world dramatically in the process. Failure in these worlds is even encouraged and many investors will not put money behind a team that has not had at least one eye-watering screw-up.

Our individual aversions or inclinations towards error have a profound impact upon our achievements and abilities to learn, change and succeed. Some people avoid making mistakes at any cost and limit their learning under the illusion of safety and security, while other people actively seek out contexts of learning that are marked by the making of multiple mistakes.

Knowing our own risk tolerance is essential so that we do not find ourselves experiencing consequences beyond our ability to respond to them safely. After all, making mistakes while jumping out of an aeroplane can potentially be fatal. Making mistakes while learning a language can come with utter delight. When we are too risk-averse we are likely to remain within our perceived comfort zones, taking less action and grabbing too few opportunities as they arise.

If you speak to any successful entrepreneur, you will usually encounter two patterns of behaviour that are dominant: consistent effort and huge risk-taking.

And it is not always the safest option to avoid putting our heads above the parapet.

Frozen-arm syndrome

A friend, Dom, offered me a good example of how our fear of getting it wrong often prevents really important action. If you happen to have been conditioned by teachers or students to avoid having a go at questions, you will relate to his anecdote.

> **Dom:** 'I only realised how crippled I was by my fear of making a mistake and bringing attention to myself when it arose in a situation where lives were potentially at risk. In my twenties, I went along to a well-known environmental campaigners' meeting, as I'd heard they needed climbers and riggers, of which I was both. The lead activist was a confident and charismatic bloke, who was worshipped by some of my friends. He started to inform us that we would be hanging campaign banners from buildings and bridges in illegal locations. He then began to expertly inform us of how to go about the process of attaching ropes at lightning speeds, so as to not get caught. People in the room

loved the idea of being spidermen and women and oohed and ahhhed at the thought of stealth rope work. The problem was that I knew that what he was proposing was so dangerous and poorly understood that it could lead to fatalities. But when he asked the room of 50 or so people if they had any questions, I wanted to put my hand up, but looked around at all the adoring faces and was paralysed by years of schoolroom training in which I learned to keep my hand down and mouth shut so as not to be humiliated if I got it wrong. Even though the voice in my head was screaming, "Yeah, I have a question, mate, how the f*ck do you think your plan will work without killing someone?"'

If you are a quiz-show fan or school kid, you will know the same rule: getting the answer right first time is what gets you points. Getting it wrong can get you a big fat zero, along with contempt and disappointment. When it comes to making mistakes, we all have our own reasons for wanting to avoid doing so. However, what I have found to be a common pattern is not so much the absolute fear of failing, but actually the fear of *not getting something right the first time.* This is quite paradoxical, because if it is your first time, it means you have no experience of it, and therefore are only likely to get it right the first time by sheer luck. If the words 'mistake' and 'failure' were changed to 'training', we might all be a little more willing to use our training in a more resourceful way. There are certainly many great benefits to be had from learning in this way.

The benefits of getting it wrong

I work with a lot of people who are crippled by their fear of making mistakes. But making mistakes can be both life-changing and fun once we learn how to approach it as such.

Bob was 11 years old and only a few short months away from starting secondary school. His parents were really concerned about his new adventure among kids he had never met before and concerned about his ability to get by in life without being ridiculed. Good-looking, dazzlingly bright, curious, athletic ... Bob had it all, including a very bad stutter. By the time his father brought him to see me, Bob had been through a number of speech therapists and stutter experts. One sin they had all been guilty of, in my opinion, was telling Bob that he 'had a stutter and was a stutterer'.

Actually, there were two sins. Despite lengthy coaching and therapy, no one had been able to ease Bob's problem.

Stuttering, along with all behaviours, is influenced by state. The idea that Bob 'is' a stutterer is a dangerous and restrictive labelling that ought to go in the bin along with many other behavioural identifications, categories and diagnoses. I asked Bob to tell me about his life. Among a number of normal, everyday boyhood activities, Bob had a deep passion for a well-known science-fiction TV show and the board games that went with it. When he spoke about general life, he stuttered and took many seconds to get his words out. When he spoke of the board game and certain characters from the show, he was able to speak crisply and clearly. If he 'had' a stutter, like having a cold, it would have been on all the words he spoke at all times. It was not and it was clear to see that Bob was 'doing' a stutter as a consequence of his state.

I asked Bob to sing a song that he knew well and he obliged easily, without stuttering. I asked him to then speak in a completely made-up gibberish and to do so for a full minute. Again, he did so easily and without stuttering. I then asked him to stand on the spot in front of my office manager and talk to her about politics for a minute. You can probably predict what happened.

I placed a pillow between Bob and myself and then stood behind him with my hands on his chest. For a full minute I matched my breathing rhythm to his. I then kept to this rhythm as I placed gentle pressure on his chest in a steady, even pace. I asked Bob to talk again about politics and as he stuttered, I increased the bellows effect on his chest to keep his breathing even. Each time he stalled to stutter, I pulled his chest in to exhale air evenly and without restriction. The result was the same as with other stutter clients. He was able to speak without the flow of air being stopped and restricted, or rather, he was *unable* to stutter. I then pulled Bob into a Third Position, so that he was looking back at the space he had just filled.

Mike: 'Do you see him breathing evenly?'

Bob: 'Yes.'

Mike: 'Can you see how easily he speaks without stuttering?'

Bob: 'Yes.'

Mike: 'You now have the choice to breathe ineffectively and do the stutter or slow your breath down to an even pace and speak clearly. What's it going to be?'

Bob started to speak with his usual stutter and stopped. He self-calibrated to his breath and then spoke slowly enough to form each word without the catch of air that had previously affected his speech. We finished and Bob went home with instructions to practise his new state-change method as much as possible.

For our second session, I asked his father to meet me in a café on a busy high street. Bob's stuttering pattern had reduced dramatically but not completely. In my initial meeting with him and his father, I noted that when Bob was asked questions he perceived to be important or when his father challenged him on a point, his breathing caught in his upper chest and he stuttered most effectively. When he was entirely relaxed and fooling around his stuttering ceased: 'behaviour is influenced by state'.

The challenge that I predicted for Bob's perfection of enunciation would be contexts where he temporarily experienced unwanted states and forgot to breathe. My strategy, therefore, was to expose Bob to a number of real-life contexts that would have the effect of firing his nervous system up, but with a guardian (me) to encourage him to retain a relaxed state.

I showed Bob a simple but effective pattern of breathing – in for a count of three seconds, holding for three seconds and then exhaling for three seconds, holding the lungs empty for three seconds, and continuing this breath cycle until a deeply relaxed state is experienced. It is important to use this pattern without forcing the breath and to have an awareness of the body in the form of the previously offered scanner – for tracking tension. Finally, peripheral vision is activated to create a state that is relaxed and alert.

Once Bob had mastered this ability to access a relaxed state, I invited him to walk a distance of 50 metres on a very busy street. The short walk was to be made in a cartoon-like, slow-motion style that would take Bob approximately 20 minutes. His instructions were simple. Stay in peripheral vision, count your breaths, release any muscular tension and do this while hundreds of people stare at you. The intention of getting Bob to do this was to desensitise him to his mind-read of what other people were thinking of him. It was also to give him 20 minutes in a mildly stressful context (for him, at least), where he could choose and manipulate his state. He succeeded perfectly, even when two separate people approached him and asked him what he was doing. His response was to stay in the relaxed state he was creating and continue without interruption.

My next task required Bob's new-state skills in a very real way. The second set of instructions involved approaching multiple strangers and pretending he recognised them as an old family friend. His job was to gush about how good it was to see them and to ask them about life. He would hold a conversation with the person for at least a minute or until I came and tapped on his shoulder. Upon hearing this, Bob tensed up and started shaking his head. I requested that he go immediately into his relaxed state, which he did with lightning speed.

My final instruction was that he was to approach strangers only in this relaxed state and stay in this state throughout each conversation. The effect was immediate. The very first person he approached was a larger-than-life street musician who ignored Bob's mistaken identity of him and instead went immediately into a philosophical conversation about his morning and how good it was to talk to people. I could not have planted a better first person to approach and Bob chatted away for some five minutes with only a small number of words being drawn out in stutter form. I interjected into the conversation with a made-up issue that I was curious to see the effect of on Bob's state.

Mike: 'Hey man, can you believe that this kid suffers from extreme social anxiety and is scared to talk to people?'

Musician: 'Yeah, I can see that!' He laughed as he spoke with an ironic tone, in response to what he probably assumed to be my equally ironic statement.

We moved on and Bob approached different people, each time becoming more relaxed and at ease with his task. One lady did indeed recognise him and told him how she remembered him as a baby. 'Hasn't time flown?' she said. Bob kept the whole charade up by constantly adjusting his physiology and breath throughout, even venturing a question on how her husband was these days? I laughed from my observer position when she told him she had never been married.

By the end of our two hours he had made multiple mistakes with a dozen or more people. We only closed the session because of my time constraints. Bob would have continued with his mistake-making all day given the chance. His stutter or rather 'state' pattern is no longer used by him and his parents tell me that he is a 'new child', in part because of the confidence he has developed from no longer being scared of getting things wrong.

Do you know anyone who is failing to achieve their potential because of their fear of failure, or fear of looking stupid, despite the promise that when the state of fear is changed, confidence is usually what takes its place?

The following exercise can be used for anyone who cares too much about what others think of them when making mistakes.

PATTERN/EXERCISE:

Become at ease with error

1. Go into a shop and buy an expensive item. Take it back within 10 minutes, ensuring that you return it to the same person who sold it to you. Tell them you made a mistake.
2. Ten minutes later, buy the item again in a different size, wait half an hour and take it back to the same sales person.
3. Repeat the first step as many times as possible, until the shop assistant refuses to sell it to you again.
4. Thank the assistant for their time and ensure that you are friendly and happy as you wave goodbye.
5. Walk up to strangers in the street and mistake their identity for someone you went to school with, or met at a party. Choose 'friendly' looking people, not mean looking.

The long game

Success and failure are two sides of the same coin. None of us knows whether today's storm clouds will drop the water for tomorrow's flowers. Success and failure are probably best played as a long-term game that can only be fully appreciated when the final whistle blows. Patience or maybe indifference throughout the game is desirable, so as not to let our score sheet affect our actions when there are still chances of a goal or two in the closing minutes.

Life is not binary with an either/or of success or failure and it is as important to be patient as it is to be diligent before judging our successes or failures, which reminds me of a little story:

One autumn day, an old man was working his field when he noticed that his old horse was sick. The man felt sorry for the horse and decided to let it pass its final days in peace. He left his horse loose to roam in the mountains and live out its final days in freedom.

Some days later, neighbours from the nearby village visited, offering their condolences, and said: 'What a pity, your only horse is gone. How unlucky you are. You must be very upset. How will you get by, work your land, and prosper?' The man replied, 'I do not know, we shall see.'

The following day, the old horse came back, now well and restored after roaming in the wild and eating fresh meadow grasses. He brought back with him nine new wild horses, which followed their new leader into the man's paddock. Word spread of the old man's good fortune and people soon visited him to congratulate him on such good luck. 'You are so fortunate!' they said. 'You must be tremendously happy!' The man smiled and replied, softly, 'I do not know, we shall see.'

At dawn, the man's only son proceeded to saddle and train one of the new wild horses. He was thrown to the ground and broke his arm. Villagers arrived throughout the day to offer their sympathy at the man's latest round of misfortune. 'Oh, what bad luck! Your son won't be of any use to you with a broken arm. You'll be required to work all by yourself. How will you survive? You must be very angry and upset!' Serenely accepting his neighbours' comments, the man answered, 'I do not know, we shall see.'

The following week, war broke out. The King's men arrived in the village, commanding that all fit and able young men were to be conscripted into the King's army. The man's son was assessed and deemed unfit because of his broken arm. 'What very God-given fortune you have!' the villagers declared as their own sons were marched to war. 'You must be happy.' 'I don't know, we shall see,' replied the old man as he walked off alone to his field.

As time went on, the broken arm healed crooked and the son was unable to use it as fully as before. The neighbours paid their condolences. 'Oh, such bad luck. This is terrible for you. You must be so angry?' The old man wisely replied, 'I don't know, we shall see.'

None of the village boys returned from the war. The old man and his son were the only able-bodied men left to work the village fields. The old man and boy became wealthy and were generous to the villagers. They said, 'How fortunate we are to have your generosity, you must be very happy?' to which the old man replied, 'It's tax deductible.'

Old men, or rather, one old man, appears in my own success/failure equation. I use a precise hallucination of a much older me, age a few hundred years (I'm betting on stem-cell treatments and a few cures to ageing) looking back and assessing what, if any, regrets I have about my life. I perceive this backward view to be accounting for a small number of operating positions I currently aim to live by:

1. I won't put off living fully today and doing what I love, for the dream of an unknown future.
2. I choose not to work with or for people I do not respect.
3. I want to spend quality time with my family every day.
4. I will live by my own standards and preferences and not be influenced by others' opinions or, worse still, popular culture.
5. I direct my attention and resources towards experiences rather than objects, therefore avoiding the strange idea that 'more stuff makes us more happy'.
6. I aim to learn something new each day that is challenging to my own positions and views.

PATTERN:

Looking back from the future

- Place two chairs a few feet apart.
- In one chair construct an image of yourself as an old person, sitting there at the end of your life.
- Sit in the opposite chair.

- Ask the older you, 'What do you regret not having done with your years?'
- Swap chairs and become the old you. Now answer your younger self.
- Sit back in your present self and listen to what the old you just said.
- Ask the older you, 'What would you have done differently if you had been without fear of failure?'
- Sit back in the older you and answer the question to your younger self.
- Ask these two questions of your older self multiple times until you are really clear about what it will feel like to have run out of time and excuses to live your life.

Who defines stupidity?

The dictionary defines 'stupidity' as: 'Behaviour that shows a lack of good sense or judgement'.

I regard this description as a bit stupid.

Who exactly defines good sense or judgement? Is it the writers of the dictionary, our politicians, or maybe God or gods? Where is the universal manual of good sense and judgement? Good sense for many of my climbing and surfing friends is never wasting more time on work than they do on play.

'Good sense' for my Republican, right-wing banker buddies is never allowing their bank balance to fall below a few million dollars.

I would like to propose (it is my book, after all) a different definition for 'stupidity' along with a description of intelligence, so as to complete both sides of the imaginary coin.

Any reader who is still bristling (just breathe and shake out that tension) from my chapter on beliefs (see Chapter 4, Freedom from the Easter bunny), may wish to turn away now.

Stupidity and beliefs share the same form of logic in my current description. If beliefs are dangerous for their bubble-like effect of blocking out new information, then I propose that they are a solid form of stupidity. In my definition of stupidity, vague, value-driven concepts such as 'good sense' do not hold up, unless you can define 'good' compared to what?

How about this? 'Stupidity is the impediment of information flow', the moat and castle of our neurology, formed to resist all invading units of new information that might otherwise topple the ruler of certainty from its throne.

The opposite of stupidity, 'intelligence', could be defined as the process of allowing a free flow of information to be received, sorted for validity, tested at the level of experience and then re-communicated to more receivers. The drawbridge is down; the doors are open, everyone is welcome for a short period of time, in which they are assessed upon real-world consequences/effects and usefulness. The ineffective visitors are then politely shown the door or simply flushed out the sewage shoot.

Over the years I have earned top marks in the globally endorsed field of stupidity. I have experienced multiple constructed and constricted versions of reality that now give me something of a benchmark to evaluate my current agnostic position against. When you have lived out as many ridiculous (or possibly correct) beliefs as I have, you will be a grandmaster of the absurd, not to tread lightly with any new position that comes along. It is preferable to tiptoe with all new ideas, suspecting that the eggshells we walk on may also have the odd welcome surprise contained within, should you happen to crack one.

One of the current views I hold is that intelligence is often prevented by our desire to remain 'right, correct or valid'. You could convert this suggestion to another: 'to fear being wrong and avoid making mistakes is just plain dumb'.

The more open we are to being wrong, incorrect or misguided, the more potential we have for upgrading our intelligence.

Be mindful

Before you recklessly run out into the world to become a master of error, I would like to make it clear that it is equally important to exercise mindfulness, or rather awareness of potential outcomes and consequences.

During the period of climbing without ropes for many years, I knew what the consequences were should I slip. At the time, the risk was still worth the experience of moving rope-free high above the ground. Fear of falling and dying just did not affect me in the way that it would now, mainly because now I view not coming home from an adventure to be the ultimate disaster for my family. Yet I, like many of my friends, still want to experience thrills and risks, as well as living long, healthy lives.

Which is why it is necessary to be able to balance the reasons for what we do with the likely results, as was apparent in the following conversation I had.

Intentions and consequences

A great friend of mine, Marcus, recently started fund-raising for a new iPhone app. His idea is brilliantly disruptive and useful and could lead to making him a lot of money. It's also a highly technical and involved idea that requires an almost 24/7 commitment to making it work.

Marcus is certainly competent enough to make this app a success, and has worked successfully on similar projects over the years. He also has young twin boys, who I know he loves to spend his every waking moment with.

In a longer conversation about his app project, I asked him about the intention and consequences of what he was embarking upon.

Mike: 'What's your intention for making it?'
Marcus: 'To solve problems for millions of people around the world.'

Mike: 'But what's your personal intention? What do you want to experience as a consequence of creating it?'

Marcus: 'I want to build it, sell it and get rich.'

I knew that Marcus already had considerable wealth and was rarely interested in money as much as other activities.

Mike: 'What's the intention of getting *more* rich from it?'

Marcus: 'Stupid question. So I can give up work and travel the world with [his wife] and the boys. Teach them to fish, sail, speak foreign languages, etc.'

Mike: 'How long will this thing take to build and how much commitment?'

Marcus: 'Maybe four or five years and a lot of late nights and weekends.'

Mike: 'Four or five years of your full-time commitment, time that you won't be spending with your boys? Do those consequences match your intention?'

After some thought, Marcus replied.

Marcus: 'No they don't, but I want to see [the app] made and realised.'

Mike: 'While also spending as much time as possible with your family?'

Marcus: 'Yes.'

Mike: 'So how could you achieve both?'

Marcus: 'I could sell the developed concept and retain a smaller percentage, and/or bring on a partner or two as founders.'

Which is precisely what Marcus is now doing, along with two founders, who share a large amount of the workload with him.

Marcus's intention for creating the app was spending every day with his family. But the consequences of creating the app in the short term (for four years or so) would mean that he was unable to experience what he really wanted on a daily basis. Which, for a business that requires his full enthusiasm for the project, is a formula for disaster.

Behind every action, there is usually an intention. The intention can exist at varying levels of logic, be it conscious: 'I want to walk to the shop to buy some orange juice because I'm thirsty', and also unconscious: 'You have low blood sugar that is directing your conscious awareness to fruit juice.'

Or your neighbours happen to be playing loud music at two in the morning. Consciously, you decide to knock very hard and loud on the wall, screaming for them to turn it down. While unconsciously you are being driven by some need for respect and to process some adrenaline that was released into your system.

I have asked my emergency-response colleagues about their reasons for heading off to disaster zones to provide aid relief. They mostly state that they intend to relieve suffering in others and provide much-needed help. But when I have delved deeper, they often admit to a need to fulfil a deeper intention, including the experiences of adventure, and the deep, fulfilling, but selfish satisfaction they get from helping others.

Once we have awareness of what we want, what we want it for and what it will cost in the way of sacrifices to get it, we are more likely to enjoy success. We can also push beyond what we assume to be our limits, welcoming the potential falls and errors to be utilised as feedback for our next set of actions.

Learning is mostly a series of small mistakes, which is why avoiding error is so counterproductive.

I could never ...

Caution and carefulness are essential to human survival, without which we would not be here today. However, fear and inhibition in physically safe contexts are unlikely to be a natural condition of human behaviour. From my observations as a father and a coach to kids, I can see that our younger friends are naturally curious and open to making mistakes. In fact, mistakes are essential for normal childhood development and only become events to avoid once previously fearless kids become inadvertently (or intentionally) conditioned by careless or fearful adults.

As a kid, you may have watched in horror as a terrified uncle gave a cringe-worthy speech at a wedding, only to decide that you yourself would feel the same terror when communicating in front of others. Maybe you have heard the words, 'What will they think of you?' too many times and now you actually answer that question as if you knew the truth.

If your physical self is not at risk, then almost any other fear of mistakes is a matter of taking life too seriously and not being open to shaking up your personal identity. If you find yourself saying, 'I could never do that', the question is 'How do you know until you are willing to give it a committed effort?'

I have noted in my work with failing business owners that the individuals who are most effective at learning and utilising what they learn are equally as effective at taking lessons and value from their mistakes. There seems to me little lost by adopting a more objective and open mind-set and seeing our failures as an opportunity to learn and investigate what could be done differently the next time.

I propose that it is high time we stopped teaching kids and grown-ups to take failure so personally. Just because you tripped on a pavement slab does not mean that YOU ARE clumsy. Losing money in a business venture does not mean YOU ARE careless. Mistakes happen and are a normal part of the experience in which we probe and test our perceived limits and understanding.

Define what success and failure mean to you and you may find that you are already experiencing more of the former than you previously imagined.

CHAPTER 7

FREEDOM FROM PAST EVENTS

The way in which we recall our memories will often affect our day-to-day choices. One bad experience in the past could, and often does, put us off similar experiences in the present ... Memories can be important for the valuable information they contain. However, when they are limiting to our lives, it's important to change their structure so that we are free from their effects.

> 'If you don't like what you're doing, you can always pick up your needle and move to another groove.'
>
> Timothy Leary

D o you remember what you ate for breakfast today? What you did last Sunday? How you spent your last birthday? When you last had an important epiphany? When you had your first kiss?

In all living creatures there is a transfer of experiences and information from our past – across time – to the present moment. We call this movement and process 'memory'. Most of us have a tendency to take memory for granted, even though every biochemical element that allows us to develop, survive and thrive in the world is dependent upon previous experiences being responded to and built upon, over and over again. From our cells up, life depends upon this constant progress of information from our past to our present, so that those experiences that lie behind us can be utilised for making decisions in the now and for what may lie ahead. Who we are today and how we interact with the world is often largely influenced by how we remember and use our past in resourceful or unresourceful ways.

For instance, when you recall a positive memory, you are almost certain to start feeling a related positive state.

For 30 seconds, try that now and fully associate with a memory by recalling a time and place in which you felt really great. To do this effectively, it is best to associate with the memory by seeing and hearing through your own eyes and ears, as if you put yourself back in time to the sensations of the past.

Did you notice how, in only a few seconds, this changed your state quite dramatically? Recalling pleasant memories is one of the easiest ways to change our state in any context in which we want a better experience.

The same also holds true for our unpleasant memories. When we happen to accidentally recall them, we get to re-experience the states that arose first time around, and in many cases, what we experience when we remember it is even worse than what we felt during the original event. This worsening effect is partly because our memories are only vaguely accurate when it comes to things such as facts.

Much of the current research on memory-processing tells us that we do not store memory as a whole unit of information to be later recalled and played across the screen of our mind. We actually store bits in different sensory locations, so that sight, sound, taste, touch and smell all have their own storage places within our neurology. The completeness of the memory gets lost with the distribution. This is why, when we remember we essentially put together pieces of a jigsaw to create a version of the past experience that is different each time we recall it. We rarely ever remember the initial complete version. More importantly, what we piece together in this moment is done in relation to our current intentions and requirements. Meaning that if I am being asked by a therapist to recall the bad events from my past, it is highly likely that I will rearrange my memories to be much worse than they actually were, just so that I satisfy the intentions of my therapeutic session.

Another striking example of how we recall information to suit the present moment is when people die. Regardless of how they lived, if we are at the funeral, we tend to remember the dead person and their activities mostly with a milder degree of judgement or criticism than we did when they were still alive. The memory fits the intention.

Just as holding too tightly to our beliefs (or indeed having beliefs at all) has the potential to create limitation in our behaviours and learning, so does believing firmly in the accuracy of our individual memories. For example, how many times have you argued with a parent or sibling over the facts of some childhood event, only to conclude that you were the only one who was actually paying attention to details at the time? While we argue about such points, it is unlikely that we will learn anything from what other people may have to say. Not that believing in the memories of other people is to be entirely accepted either! There is value in taking an agnostic approach to our memories, especially if, by doing so, we are able to release the grip on dubious facts that might limit us in the present moment.

There are useful memories and damaging memories. Without the ability to review our past, pick and choose, select and delete/overwrite what those previous experiences are, we would each become like robots, chained to our personal history and memories. It is having had learning experiences, plus the ability to review and shift portions of them, which is essential to our continuous development and self-improvement. By changing and choosing the way we experience our past, right now, in the present, we get all of the benefits of learning, without the usual limitations.

Forget me not

Imagine, for a moment, that you wake up tomorrow to find that something strange has happened to your memories as you attempt to recall them. As you search through both pleasant and unpleasant experiences you once had, you realise that all of the good memories remain intact, along with the feelings that accompany them. But, a little incredibly, when you try to recall any of the previously unpleasant memories, you do so while experiencing a neutral, or even positive, state.

On this imaginary morning, as you race through important events from your past and experience them again in some combination of your senses: seeing, hearing, smelling, tasting, touching your history, you now do so with an objectivity that you have never had before. In a moment of astonishment, you realise what this means going forward into the present and future.

1. You can now observe any part of your history and gain all of the valuable knowledge and learning from it without having your view biased by unpleasant states.
2. You can now approach and engage in present contexts that you previously avoided without fear or concern of negative, reactive behaviours being triggered by sights and sounds that are similar to some bad events in your past.
3. You are now essentially free from many of the effects of your personal history and can choose the life you wish to inhabit more precisely.

As an example, let us say that you had a terrible time at the dentist as a kid. You remember all too clearly the sound of drilling, the smell of ground bone and the utter fear and pain of the event. It was enough to put you off going to the dentist for life. Which, as a consequence, means that you now have teeth that are in need of filling, causing you pain. Hey presto, on this morning where your memories have been shifted, you are able to recall the original dentist event, including the sounds and smells (of bone), without any of the fear or pain in place. All of that fear, tension and resistance regarding dentists is lifted and you again have the choice to go and get whatever treatment you require.

More intriguing yet, after you have visited the dentist and had some work done, you realise how much your fears had transferred to other contexts, and that you are now feeling less fear about visiting the doctor and the tax man too!

Our memories can often have a debilitating grip upon us, even many years after the event. I have met and worked with individuals whose entire lives have been ruined by their regular recall of a single trauma that kept haunting them again and again. Yet, even in these worst cases, it is important to revisit and use the information contained within the memory before changing it and moving on.

Two very different stories contain the same pattern of changing our responses to bad memories. In the first story, I took a client to the place she recalled having had a terrible experience and most feared. I then dramatically changed her association with that context through less-than-conventional methods.

In the second case, I used the five-step change pattern that requires the client to hallucinate being back in the context she kept recalling. In both cases, we changed the states that were originally connected to the event with more desirable states that easily shifted the problems.

Pink dresses and phobias

Salma emailed me with an already resigned tone in her writing in regards to her phobia. She had tried years of therapy and had been to multiple specialists to fix her deep fear of escalators. One expert had informed her that her fear was linked to her father and an event with a rowing boat, which seemed very odd, in my opinion, as Salma had no issue with rowing boats whatsoever and only remembered a very scary ride on an escalator at age four.

I met Salma at my office and spent 20 minutes chatting and hearing about her regular embarrassment when having to take the stairs or lift whenever she travelled with colleagues on the London Underground. Her work for a foreign government required regular trips to London in which her teammates would travel to numerous meetings on the Tube.

I asked her to join me for a walk as we headed from my office to a busy shopping street. At that time, I had an extremely comfortable coaching office with designer chairs, cool tables and an open fireplace. What I did not have was an escalator, so we walked to the nearest one.

As we approached the moving stairs at the back of the store, Salma hesitated nervously:

Salma: 'What are we doing here?'
Mike: 'Travelling on an escalator.'
Salma: 'I can't do that.'
Mike: 'Then what did you come to see me for?'
Salma: 'I'm not ready.'
Mike: 'How do you know?'

We approached the escalator and, two feet from its base, Salma froze in her tracks, rocking back and forth. I had recently been reading a book, *Provocative Hypnosis*, by a friend of mine, Jorgen Rasmussen. When Jorgen had met with resistance from a client upon entering a supermarket, he offered an interesting ultimatum to his client that I was eager to use at least once in my life, just to observe its effect.

Mike: 'If you don't get on this escalator in five seconds, I'm going to shout at the top of my voice that you are a transvestite with an enormous erection.'
Salma: 'What? You wouldn't!'
Mike: 'Three, two, one ... [shouting at the top of my voice] ladies and gentlemen ...'

As dozens of heads turned our way, in her sudden state of panic, Salma dutifully stepped forward and stood pencil-straight and still on the escalator. I then grabbed the props nearest to me, which happened to be a bright pink-and-black-streaked dress, along with a gold-sequined shower cap that had sat on the head of a mannequin next to the escalator. I slipped the dress on, placed the shower cap on my head and called Salma's name. She turned to see me wave, as if I was the cross-dresser I had threatened to expose her as. After a few moments of staring wide-eyed in double-shock at her situation, she began to laugh. I ran up to her position and grabbed her so that we could move, in one fluid motion, to the next escalator. A mother with her two children stood just in front of us. The mother turned as I half-screamed.

Mike: 'No, no, no, I can't do it!'

The mother looked around to see me in the dress and shower cap, holding on to Salma like a small child.

Mother: (with obvious concern on her face) 'Are you okay?'
Mike: 'She's my therapist and I'm terrified of escalators.'
Mother: 'Oh …'
Mike: (to Salma) 'Will I be okay?'
Salma: (suppressing giggles) 'Yes, yes, you'll be fine.'

The lady smiled awkwardly and moved her two kids up a few steps. On the next escalator I waved at a man descending on the opposite side, offering a 'Hello handsome!' As I did, my hand accidentally brushed Salma's breast and I feigned utter horror. This caused her to erupt into yet more laughter.

By the time we arrived at the top floor, two polite security men had caught up with us and, while laughing, asked for the dress and cap back. Once again, I blamed our activities upon my therapist and she apologised as she confidently took me by the arm, guiding me around to the descending escalators all the way to the ground floor. We left the building and entered another store containing an escalator, which Salma stepped onto without any provocation.

Some weeks later, a handwritten letter arrived for me from my escalator partner. It turned out that Salma had another challenge. Riding escalators was now something she looked forward to, but her new problem was that of keeping a straight face. Every time she now rode an escalator, she broke out in fits of laughter with her new association of absurdity, which as anyone who travels on the London Underground will tell you, is far too human an emotion to be showing in public. I refrained from offering to assist her with this new response, suspecting that, in some cases, involuntary but pleasant reactions are, in fact, better than no reaction at all.

An ill wind blows

Another, much younger, client learned to connect an unpleasant state not to escalators, but rather to the sound and touch of a sea breeze.

Five-year-old Kim was tiny with jet-black hair and big, beautiful eyes. When I met her, I had an ear-to-ear grin at the sight of her china-doll cuteness, which was topped off with an accent heavily influenced by American TV. She looked and sounded as though she had come straight out of a Disney cartoon. Both of Kim's parents accompanied her to meet with me in my makeshift office that had recently had parts of the roof ripped off.

Kim's home had also recently been torn apart by the 180-mph winds of typhoon Haiyan. The family were all at home when the worst of the winds hit and her parents huddled either side of Kim as the roof and walls were dismantled around them. They survived physically unharmed. However, two days later, as they were driving with Kim in the back of their car, she heard more wind buffeting the window and reflexively dropped into a state of panic. Thereafter, each time she felt or heard more wind, she would curl her body over, squeeze her eyes closed and cease to breathe for long periods of time. Her parents had resorted to placing ear defenders on her when they walked outside, in the hope of at least limiting an auditory trigger. Unfortunately, the feeling of wind on Kim's skin also activated her panic state.

After a number of moments of shared laughter and comment to her parents that 'he's funny', I asked her, 'Shall we blow these bad feelings away?' She smiled and nodded enthusiastically. Kim was not asked, and did not mention, what she thought about when the wind touched her skin. How could she? Her nervous system's response to the memory being triggered in her neurology was one of survival. It happened so fast that her conscious mind was still at the starting line by the time her unconscious reaction was halfway around its track. With Kim in a relaxed observer position, I asked her to see (hallucinate) herself in the context that triggered her panic. She looked over to a location in the large room we occupied and then anxiously looked back to her parents and me.

Mike: 'I'm with you all the way here and we're only going to experience the bad feelings one last time. Is that okay?'

Kim nodded.

Mike: 'Kim, if you want to stop anytime, just say and we will do something that's more fun.'

I then directed Kim to walk into the position where she could see herself in the panicked state. I had no specific knowledge of what she was recalling. It may have been the night of the typhoon or her first experience in the car, or some other occurrence. What was important was that Kim was able to spatially locate and hallucinate herself in her own, unique representation of the context that triggered her panic state.

As we walked closer to the location that held Kim's hallucination of the event, her nervous system began to respond with tension throughout her body. Her attention split between her parents (possibly looking to ensure that they were still present) and the context she was viewing on the floor in front of her. She hesitated as we moved close.

> **Mike:** 'Step into the position that you see Kim in and see and hear what she sees and hears. Become her for just a few moments.'

Kim moved into position and immediately curled into a standing ball position. Her hands automatically went over her ears, her skin drained of colour and she closed her eyes. Her mother let out a small sob at the sight of her daughter reliving this moment. I waited just long enough to ensure Kim's state was activated once again as she remembered and re-experienced the events.

> **Mike:** 'Okay, Kim, you can come out now.'

She failed to hear me and so I gently touched her shoulder to bring her attention back to me. The look on her face showed real fear.

Kids are often superb at reliving past experiences and this was one that Kim had gone fully into, if the expression on her face was evidence to go by. I motioned for her to move away from her position and join me in another area of the room. I again asked her a question about a favourite moment and, before she could answer, I started jumping up and down on the spot.

> **Mike:** 'Do you like dancing?'
> **Kim:** 'Yes.'
> **Mike:** 'And jumping?'
> **Kim:** Shrugging her shoulders as if to say, 'I don't know.'
> **Mike:** 'Let's jump.'

Kim started to jump up and down and we spent a full minute shaking and moving our bodies to remove and separate from the previous sensations. We moved from the past into a clean present, without any of what Kim had just felt when revisiting the storm experience. When she was smiling and breathing faster, we stopped jumping.

Mike: 'This will be a breeze ... I'd like you to clap a rhythm that I can follow along with.'

After a little more explanation and encouragement, Kim clapped a rhythm that she was familiar with. I matched her rhythm precisely and joined her in it. I then offered the following instruction:

Mike: 'I may speed up or slow down the tempo of our clapping. The aim of the game is to follow my rhythm and keep in synch with me at all times. While clapping and when you feel ready, you can walk towards where you see and hear Kim over there [pointing to her previously located representation]. Take a walk around her and notice where she is and what she is doing. Do not attempt to change anything. When you feel ready, you can step in to where you see her and be back in the storm. If I notice that we lose our rhythm, I will stop clapping and we can move back from where you see Kim and then start again.'

Kim nodded as we began to clap.

After a small number of rhythmic rounds, I nodded and she began walking towards the location in the room where she had hallucinated and relived her memory of the event. A metre from where she had stood with her hands over her ears, her clapping rhythm faltered slightly. I asked her to step back and start again. We joined in rhythm and she repeated her slow walk towards where she was seeing herself cowering in the storm.

I mildly varied the tempo of the clapping and Kim kept pace. She walked around the area in which she viewed her panicked self. A few moments later, she stepped into the position and looked around the context she had identified. Except now, as she held our rhythm, she had no tension in her face or body. Her breath was steady and her hands were clapping and not reaching for her ears.

In this sequence of events with Kim, I used a change pattern that can be used to scrub out the unwanted states that arise from the memory of past experiences. The steps in this pattern are as follows:

PATTERN:

The rhythm of life

You will need a collaborator to work as a coach with you on this exercise.

1. From a Third Position (the observer position), select the context (we will call this context X) in which you want a difference in experience. (In Kim's case this was when she heard and felt the wind.)

2. Physically localise this hallucinated context X along with the images and sounds of yourself experiencing the behaviour you desire to change/influence. Physically visit the context X and step into it, so that you experience it from First Position (as yourself, seeing, hearing and feeling). Remain here just long enough to activate the state that is usually triggered when in context X (in Kim's case, her extreme panic).

3. Step out from context X and shake your body and jump up and down vigorously enough to shift the sensations you have just activated. This step is called a 'separator state'.

4. Start a clapping rhythm* in unison with your coach and, after five or more matched rounds, begin walking towards and around the context X.

   With your own clapping matching precisely that of your coach your aim is to fully visit context X without losing or faltering in your rhythm.

   If your coach hears any difference to your clapping rhythm, such as a mismatch, or change or falter in sequence to that of his or her own, you are to be stopped. Shake your body as per the separator state and then begin clapping again, matching your coach. The aim is enter context X, seeing and hearing all of the usual elements contained within it, while holding a steady, perfect rhythm to that of your coach. This may take multiple stops and starts, with the separator shaking and jumping in between. When you can enter the context (seeing and hearing all of the elements it contains) without losing your rhythm you have completed the pattern effectively.

* A simple rhythm of some kind, such as a commonly known version of a song or child's nursery rhyme.

As I finished working with Kim, rather than asking her how she felt, I simply opened a window. We were in one of the few rooms of the destroyed government building that still had all of its windows intact and a light breeze immediately filled the space. I beckoned Kim to the window and asked permission to lift her. I let her head and shoulders come into contact with the gentle breeze coming off the Ormoc bay.

Mike: 'How's that?'

Kim smiled and nodded her head in approval. Some two months after my return from the Philippines, her parents emailed to say that Kim had all but forgotten the event and had never again reacted badly to the sound of the wind, nor its feel upon her skin.

Here is a deconstruction of Kim's experience:

1. The wind destroys her home and her unconscious/limbic system/neurology associates the sound and touch of wind with the extreme state she was experiencing at the time.

2. Future experiences of wind act as a trigger for her to go into the extreme state.

3. Working to my instructions, Kim hallucinates in a physical location, herself experiencing the sound and feel of the wind again. She physically visits/steps into her hallucinated context and fully associates with it to trigger the extreme state.

4. Upon my request, she steps out and shakes and jumps her body to shift the unwanted state she has just experienced.

5. Kim and I now enter into the clapping pattern to generate a new state in her.

6. Kim loses her rhythm a few times as she gets closer to the location where she has hallucinated herself in the context. This proximity interrupts her state, which is displayed in her loss of rhythm.

7. Kim resets, at my request, and is able to hold the rhythm all the way into the problem context.

8. Clapping in perfect rhythm, she sees and hears the elements of the context (possibly the typhoon and the wind) as before, but now she has a new state associated with these triggers and can experience wind without her previous unconscious reaction.

What this all means

When Kim originally experienced the typhoon, it is highly likely that her primal reaction of fear and panic became associated with the sensations and sound of the wind itself. Even though the winds that came after her ordeal were gentle by comparison, they were still similar enough to the typhoon that they could trigger her heightened fear state. We all have a tendency to generalise our experiences in this way. Imagine you are on holiday, swimming in the ocean and observing an unusual ripple on the surface of the water coming towards you. Moments later, a large shark fin appears, but luckily passes you by. It makes sense, from a survival perspective, that in the future, when the water ripples, our unconscious will alert us with a huge injection of adrenaline. There is little point noting that the odds of being attacked by a shark are highly improbable. In an untrained person, once the alarm bells start ringing inside, no amount of logic can dull their chime upon the sight of a similar-looking effect on the water's surface.

It is essential that we can all sense and respond to threatening events on the rare occasions that they do arise and then swim like hell or throw super-human punches at the shark's nose. However, a problem for most people these days is that real danger rarely arrives. Instead of an event to which we can physically respond and use all of the adrenaline in our system, we get presented with challenging, but essentially safe, moments every day instead, for which our primitive fight, flight or freeze system reacts over and over again, as if we were swimming among a huge shoal of hungry predators, which we are unable to punch or to swim away from.

As logical as our conscious minds may be in some situations, many of us still run these ancient, reactive pathways of self-preservation, which seem unable to distinguish between real danger and simply the perception of it. Most of us have experienced a steady build-up of low-level stress from events such as missing trains, driving on busy roads, paying bills, moving homes or even just watching the evening news.

You may even know of someone who has a primal reaction in contexts that hardly warrant it. This may be those labelled states of panic, worry, dread, rage/anger, insomnia or just a feeling of having a nervous system that is being overly stimulated.

The neurology that once kept us safe by switching from relaxed to hyper-alert in a second, now rarely has a chance to switch back into a relaxed state, because we are endlessly responding to a world that requires attention beyond our natural ability to keep track.

Often it is useful and important to be able to fully associate with these events. Driving on busy roads at high speed is potentially fatal if we do not connect to the experience enough with our full attention. Similarly, paying bills may not have an immediate risk, but if we separate from the consequences too much, it will not be long before we are living without electricity or saying goodbye to the roof over our heads. When you think about it, bad memories and stressful events are only as unpleasant as that of the states we associate with them. Some people are able to happily remember and predict all kinds of unpleasant past and future scenarios without ever being affected. They do this by the process of dissociation.

I invite you to list one *mildly* unpleasant memory that you would usually avoid recalling, along with one future event, which when you predict it, you experience an unpleasant feeling of some kind. Use a notebook or journal to record your thoughts or write in the space below.

1. Memory:

2. Future event:

The following pattern will enable you to choose how you experience your internal versions of past events, along with changing your states to the kind you might desire to live in at all times.

PATTERN:

Memory engineering

It is initially useful to ask a friend to call out the following questions and note the answers as you first run an inventory on your memory. However, at no point are you required to tell the other person about the content of the past or future event you are working on.

1. Fully recall the mildly bad memory you previously listed, either with eyes open or closed.
2. Notice how this affects your state: where do you feel it?
3. Notice how you view the memory. Is it through your own eyes and ears (associated), or are you looking at yourself as if you are in a movie (dissociated)?
4. Is the colour lifelike, muted or something else?
5. What size are the images you see, and are they moving or static, large or small, 3D or 2D, in colour or black and white? Where is the image placed in your spatial field? Up, down, to the left or right?
6. Are there sounds or is it your own voice?
7. How are you breathing in the memory?
8. What's the temperature of this memory?

Now open your eyes, if you had them closed, and shake your body and jump up and down for 10 seconds to change/separate your state.

I invite you again to recall this memory, but this time you will choose the various elements of what you remember.

Again, it is useful to have another person assist with reminding you of the various changes to make as you go through your memory.

1. Recall the memory.
2. Notice how you feel now and as you begin to change and manipulate the elements of the memory.
3. If you previously viewed the memory and were associated with it, change your view to see yourself dissociated, as if in a movie.

If you were already dissociated when you previously recalled the memory, adjust the following elements in both instances:

1. Look at yourself in the memory from above, looking down.
2. Increase the height of your view so that you look down from hundreds of metres above.

3. Look up at yourself in the memory from floor level.

4. Float around the memory, observe yourself over the shoulder of any other person in the memory.

5. Move the memory throughout various spatial locations until it feels right.

6. Adjust the colour, brightness and contrast of the memory.

7. Change the size of the images to make them much smaller. If they are 3D, make them 2D. If they are moving, slow them down or freeze them.

8. Frame the images.

9. If there are sounds, reduce the volume or change them for sounds you prefer, such as might be heard in nature.

10. Adjust your breathing in the memory while adjusting your breath in real time. Slow your breathing down to an even, deep belly breath without tension.

11. Adjust the temperature of the memory until you find a level that feels pleasant.

12. Finally ask what valuable information or learning you might take from this memory so that the experience was useful.

As you play, test and experiment with these aspects of your memory, you will notice that by altering elements, you experience a physical shift in how you feel.

Often by recalling the memory from different viewpoints, we get to create a dissociated state that allows us to observe without feeling bad.

I encourage you to repeat the same process with the future event you wrote down above.

With regular practice of the positive manipulations of our internal imagery, the daily use of the perceptual First, Second and Third Positions, along with adjusting our breath and physiology and working with a partner to apply the rhythm process, we have a magical formula for choosing our states in the past, present and future. Which, as you will discover, has consequences that are much more than simply becoming free from our past.

Own it. Choose it

Every day, we each experience a range of events and challenges in our lives that have to be met head on. Some people do so with a smile on their faces and lightness in their step, while others make more of a meal of it.

In most instances, it matters little to anyone else how you feel while going about your daily business, just as long as you get done what is required. And yet, the way we feel, and that state we approach every task in, will influence the outcome more than anything else.

As my mentor John says:

'The problem is never the problem. The problem is the state that we approach the context where we think the problem is.'

For example:

- Your overdue bills, **regardless of how you feel**, are something you know you will pay sooner or later, and yet you allow yourself to become stressed over them.
- Your kids, **regardless of how you feel**, need attending to and caring for, even though there are days when you would like to hide yourself away in the toy cupboard.
- Your upcoming work deadline, though seemingly impossible to meet, will be met, **regardless of how you feel**, and yet you still lose sleep over it.
- The recent passing of a loved one has sent you into a deep downward spiral, one from which you never want to return. But you have a living family who need you more than those who are gone and you have to face each day, **regardless of how you feel.**
- All the money that you lost from a now-bankrupt business has the effect of making you want to throw up and curl up in a

ball. But crying and hyperventilating will not pay your rent. You have to find employment and start again, **regardless of how you feel.**

- Since saying 'I do', you and your partner have argued and found fault in every small element of each other's behaviours. You know that you need to make some big changes if this relationship is going to work. Those changes terrify you, but you are going to make them, **regardless of how you feel.**
- You are overweight. You have not exercised in years. Your health is suffering and you suspect that breaking your habits of excessive alcohol intake, eating junk food and being a couch potato will bring with it a whole set of unpleasant withdrawal pains. But you want to live past 60 and, no matter what cravings or desire for comfort you experience, you will form these new habits, **regardless of how you feel.**

In all of the above examples, and many more that we could arrive at, there is a basic condition in which we have to just 'get on with' the activities. Personally, I used to really loathe going through my receipts and paperwork. I would moan and grumble for half a day, every few weeks, about wasting my life on such things. Shopping of any kind is another activity I would avoid more than swimming with hungry sharks. However, I am required, at times, to engage in both, **regardless of how I feel.**

Why would we choose to undertake these tasks with anything other than an optimistic, resourceful state of some kind?

Where my paperwork was concerned, the real waste of my time was in my negative state, not the act of filing receipts. When I alter my images in advance of the task, as in the previous exercise, and also use Third Position, I'm actually able to enjoy a couple of hours of organising my receipts.

Once we commit to undertaking any activity, what is the use of approaching it with dread and unwanted feelings? Life is short and every minute spent on a negative experience is one that we will never get back. In addition, approaching any activity in such a state will simply ensure a poor outcome.

I am not proposing a Stepford-wife-style perma-smile and neutrality to all things. Life would be utterly devoid of diversity if we all walked around in a numb, emotion-free mode. I am all for getting giddy on joy, lost in love and high on happiness. But, experiencing negative states when alternatives readily exist in any given moment seems a poor use of our neurology. It also has the effect of creating less-than-optimum responses to our world.

Could you think of any context where positively optimising our state wouldn't be beneficial?

For example:

- If you are going to give a speech, is it best that you are in a high-performance state or a nervous, tense one?
- If you are communicating with a small child about the dangers of taking knives out of the drawer, is losing your temper as effective as gently showing the child what a knife does to a tomato if the tomato should fall (as a child might) upon it?
- If you're working with a customer, colleague or client while feeling exhausted, do you allow the tiredness to affect your interaction, or do you shift your state and responses long enough to provide a high-quality service?

Everything we do is influenced by our state, and the simplest and quickest way to adjust it is by changing our breath and physiology, using the perceptual positions and manipulating the way we organise our internal imagery. So, then, why not just do that and use these patterns to choose the way you feel, and therefore operate in the world, at all times?

I know that entire models of therapy challenge my position on the benefits of disassociating from unwanted emotions, with claims that fully experiencing our dark side, or shadow self, is important and healthy. So, let me clarify the intention of choosing our states consciously, rather than allowing the unconscious to always rise to the occasion. Under no circumstances am I suggesting that anyone should lose the choice to experience what you might label as fear, rage, shame, hate, grief, frustration, disappointment, anxiety, contempt, boredom, despair, worry, helplessness, envy, embarrassment, doubt or any other state that you sometimes experience. All of these responses, and more, should always be yours for accessing as and when we require them. There may well come along contexts and experiences in which every one of those states would stunningly serve an intention you carry or allow you to beautifully handle a difficult situation, introduce deep humour into an otherwise tense context or totally interrupt the state of someone who was about to make a horrendous mistake.

What I am offering here, in all of these methods, is *choice* and *flexibility*. If one state does not serve you well, you can simply, elegantly and speedily change it for another one that may prove to be something more desirable.

Should you be in a therapeutic process of some kind to which experiencing your dark side or repressed emotions is viewed as positive, then go for it. Only you can decide if such methods have a long-term beneficial effect. Personally, I don't want those states popping up in my nervous system on a regular basis. I share this desire for choice with a number of people who, since learning how to choose their states, have been diligent in cleaning up as many undesirable reactions as they're able to identify. This starts with noting which contexts have unsatisfactory consequences and then entering those contexts with the intention of using one or more of the change patterns available to you from this book and the app which can be on hand in emergencies. If, in context X, your neurology does 'angry', 'stuck', 'shame' or whatever, note what you can learn from that experience and then ensure that the next time you enter the same context, you do so while choosing to use the breath, internal imagery and perceptual position patterns.

There are, of course, many states that arise spontaneously and bring joy, laughter, love and a sense of freedom. I would strongly advise against interfering with those and just let them run and run.

You may have heard some people claim (without any ill intent) that their colleagues, friends, family or selves are 'shy', 'lazy', 'crazy', 'angry' and 'insolent' – or some other label. Such identity impositions come at a serious cost if either party accepts that these transient states are fixed forms of personality. I suspect that you can do 'lazy', 'shy', 'crazy', 'angry', 'depressed', 'helpless', 'envious', 'bored', and the like, as well as anyone. I want to remind you that none of those states are 'you' or your kids; they are simply responses in your neurology to past and present contexts or thoughts about those contexts; responses that, fortunately, we all have the capacity to change and choose as we see fit. We have one operating system that seems to typically experience one way at any one time. Therefore, why not choose to experience more of the states that are accompanied by a smile upon your face? I will gladly join you.

CHAPTER 8

FREEDOM FROM LIVING SMALL

Some people go their whole lives planning, working and preparing for the dream of a future that never comes. You can save yourself a lot of misery by clarifying what you really want out of life, and then experiencing the qualities of what you want each day, in some small way.

> 'We do not know enough about how the present will lead into the future.'
>
> Gregory Bateson

Regardless of how good your upbringing and education were when you were young, it is likely that somewhere throughout your life, you will have acquired at least some limiting thinking processes and behaviours that don't serve you now.

We can get an insight into what thoughts and behaviours fail to serve by how we currently experience day-to-day life, compared to what we would really like to be experiencing.

Somewhere between what we truly want and what we currently have is the gap that is mostly created by us.

If you take a moment to step into an observer position (Third Position) and view a movie-like screening of your life right now, how does it compare to the life that you once, or sometimes now, dream of?

Are you achieving your version of success in your work, romantic relationships, health, finances, family and friends, personal living environment and self-development, and would you say that you are currently inhabiting a good life that engages your best qualities, abilities and skills, or are you just cruising on autopilot while repeating mindless actions over and over again on the proverbial hamster wheel?

There are numerous reasons why people go their entire lives failing to present their best selves to the world while in pursuit of their dreams. For some (maybe the truly lucky ones), there is contentment with life at its simplest and easiest level of getting by. Not everyone desires to change the world or create a billion-dollar company, and, in fact, some world-changing, billion-dollar-company owners dream of nothing more than simplifying and achieving contentment with far less.

Some people seem to be lucky and know what their life purpose is from an early age. They then commit their whole lives single-mindedly to this, without (seemingly) any consideration for alternative paths.

Other people may wonder, too long, what their calling or greatest achievements could be, and in doing so they keep wondering until they get old and eventually die, with their songs still unsung inside them.

But what if you really don't know how your own song goes? Or what your life's eventual masterpiece might look and feel like? And even if you think you know, can you be sure that such wants are not simply a response to the endless input of advertising and cultural suggestion that a perfect life looks like a big house, with a sports car and a Rolex?

I know from my own personal experiences of reading best-selling motivational books in my early twenties that I placed the wrong form of goals at the end of my carrot-stick. In business, cash flow is everything. But I cared little about making money and only about going on adventures or studying nutrition and fitness. My values and intentions were far from aligned with the daily requirements of running a business to make money.

Hence why my early ventures into nightclubs and then sports marketing were doomed from the start.

I cannot emphasise enough the importance of checking that your intentions are aligned with the actions that are required to get you there. Failing to do so often creates many problems along the way, regardless of what the end success could be. You may even be able to ignore the everyday discomfort that your unconscious provides for your hard efforts. Some people can seemingly work their whole lives feeling resistance to what they do and yet still eventually achieve their intended outcomes. However, those people who seem to effortlessly get what they want, will first clarify their intentions and then ensure that the consequences (what they experience as good and bad) of their actions are aligned with that intention.

A friend of mine recently invested most of her savings and some loan money in a coffee shop because she a) loves coffee and b) loves sitting and chatting while drinking in coffee shops. Had she asked herself her intention for wanting a coffee shop, she would have clarified that she wanted to spend time hanging out in her favourite kind of place, socialising with people.

As a new owner of a coffee shop surrounded by many other cafés in her area, do you think that is what she currently does? Last time we spoke was because she needed help with her stress. The business requires her to work six days a week just to cover the rental costs. Sure, she gets to sit and drink coffee during quiet periods, but while worrying about not having enough customers.

Day to day as she works hard to prevent losing her investment she rarely gets to enjoy a moment of being aligned with her desire to socialise in a relaxed fashion.

Be here, now

Have you ever asked why we dream in the first place when it so often leads to disappointment and regrets?

I don't know about your dreams specifically, but it seems mostly that when we dream (as in 'aspire to'), we get to predict certain qualities that are not being experienced in the present. When writing this book in the depths of a cold, dark British winter, I was hidden away in a sleepy little hamlet and my dreams contained sunshine, warm ocean and wide-open spaces; a great distraction from my reality, as are all dreams. Upon arriving back at my home in the USA in July, the missing elements of my life that were in those winter-time dreams were in some way met by living a short drive from the Pacific Ocean and being able to get in the water and surf for an hour each day. Images that stirred me to momentary discontentment ceased and no longer called to me. I know when I am living aligned with what is important to me – dreams of another place or life no longer arise randomly from my unconscious, because I am actually living in a way that matches my needs.

Karl Marx made the claim that 'religion is the opium of the masses', which is an apt reminder that our dreams can come at the cost of our present lives.

We can work our backsides off for some distant day that holds the promise of qualities we currently live without. But as may be the case with living a restricted, pious, religious life for the reward of eternal happiness, the longed-for gates of heaven could end up not being there at all. Similarly, some people work their entire lives to achieve an idea of happiness forged from material gain, only to find that happiness is far from connected to the size of a house or the make of a car.

I am all for dreaming big and using a dream for direction and getting the best from ourselves, but I would advise against doing so entirely at the expense of what you could currently be experiencing.

It may well be one of the strangest and saddest glitches of the human nervous system that so many of us are gladly willing and able to sacrifice the beauty, the wonder, the love, the joy, the health and the happiness of today, for some version of all those qualities in an entirely uncertain future, especially when there is another way.

I encourage you to put this book down for a few minutes and go and write down in your notebook or journal what it is that your dreams hold for you that your current life lacks?

You may say that, in your dreams, you have unlimited wealth and riches. Maybe that would be great for many reasons, but what inner experience does this give you beyond physical stuff that you do not, or cannot, already experience a version of in some way now?

You may say that being gloriously wealthy is a better way to live than being poor, and I would mostly agree with you (though the happiest humans I have met often live with few possessions or money). However, becoming gloriously wealthy at the cost of not living fully in your limited days, weeks and years is surely too high a price to pay.

Maybe it would not be such a gamble if you could guarantee your actual time alive on the earth, along with a guarantee that you will get what you want and that when you do, it delivers on its promise of happiness. But, really, can anyone guarantee such predictions? Of course they can't.

Which is why, if you want to experience spontaneous states of contentment, happiness, joy and delight, I suggest pulling apart those future compelling dreams and asking, very honestly and specifically, what each dream contains that is missing in this moment? I do not mean that what is missing is a yacht or a gold watch. I mean what states do you assume the yacht or gold watch might generate for you?

You may assume that such objects will provide the ticket to feelings of pride, freedom, confidence, respect or whatever. But, as you know from reading this book, such states are fleeting, and, more importantly, can be experienced without the need to have a physical object as a reminder to do so.

My urgent question is, 'How can you experience what you want in some future day – now, in this moment, while working your way to that dream outcome?'

Once you know how your dreams are signposting the missing elements of your current existence, you can go about restoring those missing parts to begin living fully with presence and dignity.

But you might say, 'I really do want that yacht and a million dollars in my bank account.'

'So what will the yacht give you that you don't have available to you right now?'

'It will give me freedom and the open sea. Freedom from this job that I hate, this place that I loathe, this drudgery that I abhor.'

'Do you really think it requires a yacht and a million dollars to move firmly away from your present conditions?'

If you're a parent, like me, you likely want to provide everything you can for your kids, maybe including the best things and the best education.

Providing for our kids is often enough justification to commute every day to a high-stress job that we would gladly leave tomorrow if we could. After all, one day your kids will, hopefully, appreciate all the hard work you put in and all the home-life moments you sacrificed to provide them with their stuff and their education.

But it may be worth noting that one day, all of those special, magical, irretrievable days of childhood will be gone forever, with only snippets of memory from a few holidays, during which you possibly switched your work emails off and paid full attention to your child's beauty for a fleeting moment or two.

If you're not a parent, you will still know of experiences that really matter to you which you sacrifice every day to chase your future goals. I like to ask my clients how much of their life, when quantified in time, energy, health and meaningful experiences, is worth the things and future outcomes they are chasing?

For all of us, there are far greater costs being paid than the fees of expensive schools, handbags, watches, cars and other spoils. We pay for everything in some way with the life we have, which is limited and worth guarding far more than many other things.

I am not suggesting that we all become Tendai monks, living only for the next footstep around a sacred mountain, or a jungle shaman, living at the pace of forest life. Most of us can benefit from planning our lives and designing a bright future to compel us forward.

As a climber, I am aware of how important it is to successfully get to the summit of a big mountain, by using a degree of pre-planning and applying disciplined attention and practice in preparation. However, if that disciplined practice requires us to live only for the hope of a summit called 'tomorrow', is it really worth it? Is it not better to fully live today and every day with a slower and more enjoyable approach to our chosen summits?

The biggest irony of chasing future dreams without our self-dignity intact in the present, is that we are less likely to create what we want in the future. Today's actions are like seeds planted for an unseen harvest yet to come, therefore it is surely better if we ensure that today's sowing contains the fullness of who we are and what we can experience presently.

If we choose our dreams wisely so that each new day contains at least a small part of them, we are more likely to experience motivation, enthusiasm and drive in abundance, which will make the adventure of going after our biggest visions all the more fruitful.

What's the smallest step?

You may want to create results in your finances, health, career, family/friends, romance, intelligence, self-development and many other categories. When you dream of your future greatness, you likely view success in all those areas of life, and more, and you would be right to do so. However when we chase too many dreams, we can often be left short in all of them. I've worked with highly motivated and talented individuals who want to be world-class in everything they do. It's a laudable aim that can often come with the consequence of being spread too thinly to really achieve what is wanted.

It's useful to be specific about our goals and outcomes, by choosing categories and contexts in which to focus our efforts. Wanting to be 'successful' or 'rich' or 'healthy' is too abstract an outcome for directing our actions with the smaller steps that will create it. So get specific by creating strategies in small, manageable chunks.

Some people are really good at dreaming up big ideas, with little consideration for the details, while others are great at details but lack the capacity to think big. Most successful people either have a capacity to think in both ways or they hire other people to think for them. This pattern of thinking both up and down, known here as 'chunking', is useful in most of our daily activities and, when practised regularly, can be applied with positive effect to everything you do.

As an example of 'chunking down' into specificity, I offer a common example of wanting and making food.

- What food specifically? A salad.
- Chunking down from salad, I list the multiple ingredients: lettuce, onion, tomato, cucumber, avocado, etc.
- Chunking down again, I can say that those ingredients will provide vitamins, minerals, fibre, etc.

I will also need to undertake certain actions to put the salad together:

- 'Make the salad' breaks down into:
- Choose ingredients.
- Locate the sources of these ingredients.
- Purchase the ingredients.
- Return to my kitchen with the ingredients.
- Prepare the ingredients.

- Mix the ingredients.
- Arrange the salad on plates or put it in a bowl.

We could also break each of the above actions into smaller subsets of actions. For example, under 'choose ingredients':

- List the multiple ingredients below it, source a pen and paper and a location to write in and Google 'mixed salads' to provide ideas for ingredients.

We can specify as we chunk down to the tiniest elements of the activity, which then gives us precise and usable starting points.

'Chunking up' has the effect of being more abstract and is discovered by questions such as, 'What is the purpose of this and what is this a part of?' In our salad example, we might answer 'interacting with our environment' (eating is arguably the closest interaction we have), 'creating sustenance', or even 'connecting with nature' or 'doing what I love'.

The process of dividing information into specific chunks allows us to create a more detailed map of how we can best achieve the results we are looking for. Chunking is also useful for preventing a sense of being overwhelmed when confronted with large quantities of new information. You could view yourself as an engineer creating a design map of what you dream of achieving.

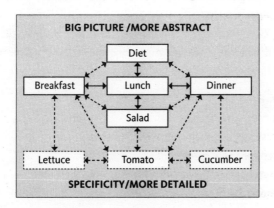

Choose an outcome and more than one way to get it

It can be good to remind ourselves that life is a journey of many miles that have to be completed at each step. The more focused, attentive, committed and resourceful we are to those small steps, the more likely our outcomes will be as we want them.

Before committing an ounce of effort to your future, simply choose a category in which success is wanted, and then apply the intention/consequence question to it.

'What is my intention for achieving this?'

'What are the likely consequences (positive and negative) of my actions that will be required to achieve this?'

'Do the consequences of those actions match my intention?'

As an example, someone who wants to achieve a better social life might go to bars and drink a lot. The intention is to enjoy the company of people, but the consequences are inauthentic behaviour and poor health. Neither of which fulfils the original intention.

I offer an example of a mismatch in intention from a 50-year-old man who wanted me to coach him to achieve his goal of promotion – we spoke for 10 minutes and I have shortened the answers to the relevant parts.

> **Mike:** 'What specifically are you aiming for? By specifically, give me a description of what you will see, hear, feel when you have this promotion?'
>
> **A:** 'To become one of the managing directors at work. I'll be one of the bosses, with the whole division under my direction and I'll have the responsibility of driving our business to greater growth and fame. I'm seeing my office, my team, hearing voices of people who work for me.'
>
> **Mike:** 'What's your intention for achieving this outcome – what do you want to experience when you achieve it?'
>
> **A:** 'Uh, I've never thought about that … [after a minute of thinking] … I'll feel successful and in control of my life.'

Mike: 'In what other contexts do you feel successful and in control?'

A: (More extended thinking) 'I'm not sure that I do feel successful or in control … uh, maybe when I'm playing squash, which I'm very good at.'

Mike: 'What evidence do you have that becoming the boss will give you the feelings of success?'

A: 'It's the dream, isn't it? Being the boss and captain of the ship.'

Mike: 'Whose dream?'

A: (Silence …) 'I thought you were meant to motivate people?'

Mike: 'When people are in alignment with their dreams, they rarely need motivating. Are the everyday actions required to achieve this goal in alignment with your intention? Will you feel successful when you are in the process of getting to be MD?'

A: 'I will have to work a lot more for the next few years and that would mean having less time with [partner's and kids' names], and there's no guarantee of getting the promotion, of course.'

Mike: 'Is the necessary extra work in alignment with this goal of wanting to experience success and control?'

A: 'Successful people have to work hard to get what they want.'

Mike: 'Success is best when it's self-defined. Do you know of any successful people who don't work more hours than they want?'

A: 'Yes' (mentions names of people he knows).

Mike: 'In how many other ways can you experience the state of success and control without becoming MD?'

A: 'I don't actually want control. But success, I guess, is working in doing what I love … It's not about money for me.'

Mike: 'Is doing more of what you love achievable?'

A: 'Yes [laughing], if I worked less and put time into my other passions.'

Mike: 'Is that other work in alignment with your intention of feeling successful?'

A: 'Yes, totally. I'd love to work in [names motorbike-related subject].'

Mike: 'Can you identify three more ways of feeling successful that don't require becoming an MD?'

A: 'Yes, most likely.'

Mike: 'So you have the choice now of how to get what you really want, which is the experience of success.'

A: 'Damn, maybe being the MD isn't what I'm looking for ... '

There are always multiple ways to fulfil the intentions we hold. However, all too often what we assume to be the correct actions have consequences that are far from what we want.

PATTERN/EXERCISE:

Intention/consequence

Ask: What is my intention behind X behaviour?
Ask: What consequences (positive and negative) do I experience as a result of the current behaviour?
Explore: What are three alternative behaviours or actions (other than the present behaviour) that will satisfy this intention without the negative consequences?

Jack and the granite beanstalk

One of the greatest experiences of my life was working with my friend Jack Osbourne and being a part of his televised transformation. Over a period of six months Jack, my wife and

I were able to test and verify a number of important strategies for achieving a genuinely remarkable goal.

> **Jack:** 'Mike, I think we should go down, it's just not going to happen, we've nearly run out of food and we're barely halfway up the wall. This is way harder than I ever could have expected.'
>
> **Mike:** 'Then you should have expected more. At what point did I suggest it would be easy?'
>
> **Jack:** 'You didn't, but I haven't slept, we're all starving, and going too slow.'
>
> **Mike:** 'Think about everything you've gone through to get to this point. Are you willing to throw that away? And do you really think two or three more days of effort is going to break you?' Long pause …
>
> **Jack:** 'No, it won't break me. And you're right. I just haven't slept all night and feel like shit. [Nodding in acceptance] Let's get the coffee on.'

Like many people, you may have some doubts about your ability to achieve a certain task at some point in your life. The above conversation with my friend Jack had plenty of background evidence to support his side of the argument. We were 1,500 feet up El Capitan, the behemoth granite wall in California's Yosemite Valley, filming a TV series about Jack's transformation from celebrity nerd to muscled adrenaline junkie. Our team of three climbers, two camera riggers and one cameraman had been on the wall for four days and were not yet at the halfway mark. We'd rationed enough food for five days and were all eating less than 1,000 calories while burning five or six times that amount. If nothing else, it was a great way to lose weight!

The problem we faced was a matter of sequence in our climbing. Our riggers first went to put ropes in place for the cameraman. They then ascended the ropes and filmed while we started climbing. The issue was that of all the climbers on the wall, I was the fastest at lead-climbing, but was spending half a day waiting for our riggers to put the ropes in place so I could be filmed. As any good chess player knows, strategy is everything and ours sucked.

Getting to this point on the wall had been quite a journey in itself. Six months before, Jack had been 40 kilos overweight, unable to rise from bed before midday and so unfit that an initial 20-minute jog on the beach turned him into a heaving, panting wreck, all at the tender age of 19. I lost count of the number of friends who sniggered and smirked when we told them of our aim to help Jack transform into an amateur adventure athlete, with the final task of ascending one of the most iconic and difficult rock faces in America.

I was considerably more confident than my friends about our challenge, because I knew that when Jack agreed to the undertaking, we had five essential conditions on our side that would enable us to achieve our goal:

1. **It was compelling.** Ours was such a huge and unlikely challenge that whenever any of us thought about it, we had a visceral feeling. Meaning that it was not just a nice little idea to talk about, it actually set our nervous system alight with a mix of fear and excitement. We also knew that if we could successfully transform Jack from being overweight and unhealthy, we could inspire thousands of other people in the process.

2. **The intention matched the consequences.** To achieve our goal of climbing the kilometre-high rock face, Jack had to practise climbing, martial arts, healthy eating and a bunch of other really compelling activities. The actual process in itself was, mostly, one that motivated us all each day. The final goal of summiting held the promise of utter satisfaction and a huge sense of achievement, which all of our daily actions were aligned with. If we made it, we also knew that we'd be sending a positive message out to everyone who watched the show. All aspects of why and how we wanted to do it were aligned.

3. **There was risk and jeopardy.** Every hour of our journey was filmed and ultimately millions of people would know if we failed when our efforts were televised. We would also fall short of our aim to inspire countless kids to commit to something that was seemingly impossible.
4. **We were a team.** Jack had two completely committed friends who were ready to do almost anything to achieve the huge task and though we all had our challenges and down days, we supported each other to the very end.
5. **We knew how to provoke change.** Certain words, statements or small actions had the effect of getting all of our team into a more positive and resourceful state. Provoking changes in each other's states was an essential ability we all learned from living side by side for so long.

By day four, at the 1,500-ft point of 'El Cap', Jack had trained and fought with traditional Thai fighters, climbed ice walls in the Alps, run countless mountain trails, climbed thousands of metres of rock faces, trained thousands of press-ups, sit-ups and squats and eaten far more fruit and vegetables than pizza and ice cream. All through his own hard work, sweat, blood and many tears.

What struck me as crazy at the point where Jack and the rest of our team were considering dissent through descent, was how easy it was for them to give up when they were so near the finishing line.

Up to that point, Jack had thrown himself into the deep end with metaphorical whirlpools and sharks and survived each time. Not only that, but he had thrived after each new event of which he had previously been 'shit scared' and convinced of certain failure.

In fairness, when you have been an overly protected kid for most of your youth and an example of living small, it can be quite a task to shift from fear and trepidation to courage, curiosity and congruency. This is when the ability to change our states as easily as we might change a jacket is essential for a successful outcome.

Jack and the crew decided to catch up on some serious sleep deprivation. This meant that the two strongest climbers could move rapidly and lightly up the many pitches of rock that separated our team from success. My climbing partner, Steve, and I forgot all about making TV shows and instead spent glorious hours doing what both of us loved, climbing, for the pure joy of it. By the time night was drawing in, we had covered many hundreds of metres of vertical rock face and knew that from our high point of the day, we could make it to the top with only one more full day of climbing to go.

Jack and the team caught up on sleep and enjoyed just hanging out on a big ledge, making the most of the view. The rest restored their enthusiasm and they followed us up the rock with ease.

Thirty-six hours later, the last 40 metres of climbing was led and completed by Jack, so that he was the first of our team to stand on the summit. Six months earlier, he would not have had the fitness or ability to even walk the winding paths to that high spot.

If you are going to put time, effort and resources into achieving your dreams, you can make your success a lot more likely by using the similar strategies that we did when turning an out-of-shape kid into a competent adventurer. Those strategies are important enough to repeat once again:

1. **Make it compelling.** Take a look at your goals and dreams right now. Do they give you a feeling of excitement and anticipation? Are they motivating in, and of, themselves? If not, and you predict that you will need exterior motivation, this is probably not the goal or dream for you. However, if when you think about your goals and dreams, the effect is compelling to the point of excitement, and it inspires you to want to give everything else up to achieve it, I offer this advice, 'double it'.

   That's right, double the size, scope and scale of what you conceive of achieving and then experience how that affects you when you see it this way.

It is likely that any future you can conjure is possible if you have given full congruency towards making it happen. By congruency I mean that your conscious and unconscious focus and direction are undivided and there is no tension between what you think you want and what you feel you can achieve. (See the peripheral ball game on page 198 to enable unconscious congruency.)

2. **Ensure that your intention matches the likely consequences.** Every action counts. Check that your efforts are not misaligned with what you really want. There are always multiple ways to achieve your intentions, so do not get fixed on one outcome.

3. **Build in risk and jeopardy.** In my mid-twenties, I set up two businesses with my own money. However, I was not ready for the day-to-day commitment of running a business and got into the habit of going climbing at the first sign of good weather. I also did not care all that much about losing my entire savings, because it does not cost much to climb rocks, which was really when I was at my happiest. Some years later, when a friend invested in my business, everything changed. Knowing that I was working with other people's money, and that they trusted me, meant that I pretty much gave up climbing altogether to make those business ventures work. If you have no risk of loss involved in your dream, you may find that it is too easy to let it slide. Tell everyone who will listen, get others involved, make big, bold statements about your intentions and burn your bridges. Being only partly committed to any project will rarely deliver the results you desire.

4. **Build a team.** When you look back at all of your minor and major successes in life, it is likely that you will notice a number of people who formed a part of what you did. Few of us can truly say that we achieve much without the help of others. You may want to get in shape after years of over-eating. Won't it be easier with your family and friends supporting you in your efforts? You could also take the simple step to find a group of like-minded newbies so that

you can all encourage each other. Or you might be starting out on a business venture in which you will need multiple experts in accounting, managing, marketing and more. Before you do, I would say it is invaluable to find a mentor, or some model of excellence in your intended field, a person who can shortcut all of the mistakes you might make if you were starting out with no experience. Even if your dream is to find love, it will be easier when friends are supporting your quest with invites to dinners to meet potential dates. Regardless of what you are working on, find the very best people you can. Tell them passionately about your plans and allow them to share in your dreams in a way that works for their own intentions. More importantly, give them your support and become a part of multiple teams to get your friends and colleagues closer to their dreams as well.

5. **Know how to change states.** As with all activities, the states in which we approach the task/context will influence our success or failure. Pay attention to creating the most resourceful states for the task in hand and the high-quality actions will follow.

The next pattern/exercise works by building a high-performance state while approaching and stepping into an outcome in which you desire an enhanced state. You will need six tennis balls and two other people (one player and two throwers) to play.

PATTERN:

Peripheral-vision ball game

1. The player focuses approximately 2–3 metres ahead on a physical location (the outcome space) in which he/she sees and hears herself in a future goal/outcome.
2. Two partners (the throwers) will be passing balls to the player. The throwers stand approximately 1–1.5 metres to

the left and right sides of the player at a 10 and 2 o'clock angle to the player's 6 o'clock position.

3. The throwers begin to pass the balls to the player, and the player catches the balls and then throws them back. Balls thrown on the left side are caught with the left hand; balls thrown on the right side are caught with the right hand. The throwers begin to move further away from the player so that they are in the player's peripheral vision. They also increase the speed of throwing, only if they calibrate that the player is increasing in effectiveness as their performance state builds.

4. As the player's state builds (as observed by the throwers from the flow and ability to catch and pass the balls effectively without dropping or displaying tension) a (pre-assigned) thrower tells the player to walk towards the hallucinated outcome space while still catching and throwing the balls.

5. As the player moves towards the outcome space with the state building, they eventually step into where they see and hear themselves. Without any conscious effort, they now associate the performance state with their future outcome.

Spectacular you!

Maybe it is just me, but when I observe a small baby, I see a blank slate on which a million potential visions of greatness can be painted. Similarly, when I observe world-class adults, I wonder what kind of a child existed in that person's beginnings. And, most of all, I wonder how the highest achievers and examples of human excellence got to where they are and how their strategies could be used by the rest of us.

For most people who have never competed in a sport, if you look at the Olympics or other examples of world-class physical performance you will observe humans, seemingly from a superior species, who can sprint, jump, lift, fight, balance, row, swim, throw and execute levels of prowess that induce awe, wonder and respect.

If you were to experience a world-renowned orchestra playing you would know, from the first notes, that you are in the presence of multiple creative geniuses implementing their art with utter, absolute precision and timing so that a millisecond of discordance would sound like a smashing glass.

In art, some professionals can transfer information from real life onto a flat canvas in such a way that it leaves us wondering which is more real?

Mathematicians and physicists can work on equations that are so complex, so abstract and yet so precise that they can provide insights into the very nature of our universe, all by pencilling symbols upon a page.

We do not have to look far to see that our world is full of extraordinariness that comes from focusing our attention and actions onto what is important to us.

Extra ordinariness.

But what is the extra that takes us beyond the ordinary?

Most people know, with absolute certainty, that they will never break an Olympic record of any kind. However, when you watch Usain Bolt thrash his competitors in the 100-metre sprint, despite being the wrong size and shape for his particular sport, it is time to admit that it is only excuses that get in the way of us experiencing freedom from living small. Achieving more in all our endeavours is a matter of applying more attention and more effective actions towards them. There is a reason why you may not be great at sprinting, or playing a musical instrument, speaking a second language, programming a computer, juggling, painting, dancing tango, experiencing meaningful relationships, or eating gourmet home-cooked food.

You simply do not put your attention and practice into those areas.

We can think about what we want all day long, but until our daily actions are directed towards our dreams, the bridge between now and what we desire in the future will forever remain un-built.

You are made of the same stuff as an Olympic athlete, a world-class musician, a mind-blowing artist, a top CEO, a ground-breaking scientist and all of the other examples of excellence in the world.

You may believe that you are too old, too poor, too black, too white, too short, too fat, too stupid or some other unfounded belief that prevents you from transforming and reinventing yourself. What really counts, regardless of where you are right now, is to check that your actions are fully aligned with the intention you have for your life. If they are not, it is never too late to stop what you currently do and instead come up with a number of alternative behaviours and actions that serve you better.

I know of individuals who have been trained from the earliest of ages to accept limiting belief systems about how the world really is. Yet regardless of how strong an influence such training exerts, there is always the opportunity to drop the past and go in search of different versions of reality. Even if that means leaving behind everything you have ever known and been supported by, as my friend courageously proved to me a year after first meeting him.

Caller: 'You're not going to believe this … Are you ready?'

Mike: 'Tell me, big guy?'

Caller: 'I … HAVE … A … GIRLFRIEND!'

Mike: 'Holy crap, that didn't take long! Where and when did you meet her?'

Caller: 'I met her last week at one of the classes I've been going to. She's Polish and beautiful and smart and … it's amazing.'

Mike: 'When you say, "It's amazing", what exactly are you talking about?'

Caller: 'It – SEX, it's the best thing ever. It's, it's …'

I interrupted.

Mike: 'Yeah, I know what it's like, man. You can keep the details to yourself [pause]. I couldn't be any happier for you. How's everything else going?'

Caller: 'Not so good. I don't have any money since my friend fired me. He's not returning my calls either. It's been a real lesson in how people are in the real world.'

Mike: 'Hang on, he told me he'd look after you and that you were sacred to him. Like, SACRED. Now he's fired you?'

Caller: (laughing) 'Yes, I guess I don't hold the ticket to his eternal happiness any more!'

Mike: 'What a cretin.'

Caller: 'It doesn't matter, Mike. I'm happy. For the first time since I can remember in many, many years, I can honestly say I'm happy.'

Mike: 'What's the best of it? Other than sex, of course?'

Caller: 'Just being able to walk around London as a normal person. To speak to people – to speak to women in a normal way, to buy coffee with cash, to visit historical locations, to go to the movies, to eat ice cream and drink a glass of wine. I doubt you will ever appreciate just how incredible all these things are.'

Mike: 'I hope you washed your hands a hundred times after paying for the coffee?'

Caller: (squealing with delight) 'I would need to fast for a lifetime to purify from my recent activities!'

Mike: 'Have you had any correspondence from the organisation or your guru?'

Caller: 'No. That is the hardest part. I never believed for a second that they would simply delete me from their world after 28 years of service. Even my so-called best friends only seem to be friends when the hope of enlightenment or karmic elevation is on offer.'

Mike: 'Like I said, Swami, they're cretins.'

Caller: 'You have to stop calling me Swami. I told you what my new name is, so use it or I'll kick your ass!'

Mike: 'Man, you've developed some serious attitude since we met.'

Swami: (laughing) 'I'm making up for lost time.'

Ask better questions

If my client-turned-friend was able to step away and reinvent himself after 22 years of strict conditioning, living as a holy man, I am mostly sure anyone can.

Whenever we face challenges that initially seem too big or beyond our reach to overcome, we can ask two simple but highly effective questions:

1. What stops me?

and

2. What does it take to get there?

In your own life, you might answer the first question by saying that you do not have the time, money, support, energy, know-how or some other 'reasons'.

My second question in response to such answers is, what does it take to get those elements in place? When answering this question, consider only what is within your own capabilities to make it happen. Do not factor in luck, random events or the assumption that other people will take responsibility for your needs. Winning the lottery is not an event that is within your capacity to effect, unlike learning a type of new skill or ability that has been proven to move you closer to what you want.

Whatever you assume to be the limiting factors in achieving your dreams, they are only that – assumptions. Nowadays, a young person with a smartphone in rural Africa has more access to information than Bill Clinton did while he was President of the United States. The Internet and the information we access through it has dramatically changed the way we learn. If you want to know how to start a company, manage your time, raise money, build a team, get well, write a book, create a brand, simplify your life, start a pop group, or pretty much anything you can conceive of, the knowledge on how to do so is right there at your fingertips. But what the Internet is not able to do (yet?) is to enable you to move your muscles into action and get things done.

The reality is that a lot of people read books (like this one) or consume online content and then do pretty much nothing with the information. Yet it's clear that the difference that makes the difference between world-class performers and regular folks is the degree of their congruent commitment, paired with almost constant action.

The majority of people who achieve what they want in life, do so after facing countless challenges, because most achievements that we value don't come easily.

When you desire to stop living small and live a fuller, more rewarding, life there will likely be bumps and dips in the road. This is when having effective ways of overcoming our perceived difficulties becomes essential.

In my own life I use the patterns within these pages every day in one context or another as I work on my various projects. I also have a go-to pattern for any context in which I am having a less than optimal experience.

I have personally played the 'Alphabet Game' hundreds of times, and many thousands more with clients. The beauty of this game is that though a coach can ensure an optimal application of the game, it can also be effectively played solo. I have a version of the game's chart on my office wall and will use it any time I may be performing below par.

The application of the game is the same as in previous chapters, where:

1. From Third Position, the player first identifies some context (we will call 'x') in which they want a different, more enhanced, experience, and then they physically locate that context (x) near them, observing him or herself in it.
2. The player visits the hallucinated context and sees and hears as if in it (associated) until the states connected to that context are experienced.
3. The player steps out and shakes their body enough to separate the state experienced in the context.
4. Play the game (see instructions below), in this case the Alphabet Game.

5. At a stage when a high-performance state is activated, the player steps back (re-visits) into the context (x) with their neurology fully activated.

PATTERN:

Alphabet game

You will need a large (preferably poster-sized) sheet of paper and a marker pen.

Copy the following code onto your paper:

a	b	c	d	e
l	r	t	t	l
f	**g**	**h**	**i**	**j**
r	r	t	r	t
k	**l**	**m**	**n**	**o**
l	r	t	l	r
p	**q**	**r**	**s**	**t**
l	t	l	l	r
u	**v**	**w**	**x**	**y**
t	l	t	r	l

You can copy the above chart verbatim. However it is important to change the sequence of letters below the alphabet line every few plays. This is because our neurology gets used to the pattern and consequently becomes less stimulated by its effects.

To write new letter sequences there are two rules:

1. Never repeat a letter more than twice in a row, ll, rr, or tt is fine. However lll, rrr, or ttt is not.

2. Place l (for left) under r in the alphabet line, and r (for right) under l in the alphabet line. Under t in the alphabet, place t (for together).

Stage 1: The top row of each line of letters contains the English alphabet.

The player begins at the letter 'a' and finishes at 'y', calling out the alphabet in sequence. As the player calls out each letter, they simultaneously raise the corresponding arm: l for left, r for right and t for both hands together.

Repeat this several times, solo or preferably with a partner, who can observe whether you are playing correctly. Spend approximately two to three minutes on this first stage.

Stage 2: Begin at the letter 'y' and move backwards through the alphabet towards the letter 'a', calling out each letter and lifting the corresponding hand. Spend approximately two to three minutes on this second stage.

Stage 3: Is similar to stage 1, with one addition. As the player raises his or her hand, they simultaneously lift the opposite foot and leg (i.e. moving left arm and right leg; right arm and left leg). When lifting both arms they make a small jump, or for players with any joint or knee issues, they can dip the hips. When the player runs from 'a' to 'y', they then reverse the order, back and forth. Spend approximately 10 minutes on this final stage.

For solo players who do not have a coach to assist them, I recommend setting an alarm for this final stage. As soon as the alarm goes off after 10 minutes, move immediately from the game into the context (x) in which you desire more choice. Move without hesitation or pause from the game to the context (x) so that you can connect the newly generated high-performance state with the stimuli (sights and sounds) that previously signalled a low or non-resource state.

When played effectively the stimuli that previously activated unwanted states will now re-activate the high-performance state the player just generated from the game.

One superbly effective way of using this game is to identify a new context every day in which you have a less-than-optimal experience. Apply the five-step change process with the Alphabet Game played at step 4. If, for a month, you put 15 minutes aside each day to run the full pattern, you will experience a deepening of choice in all of the contexts you apply the game to, as well as many more that share similar qualities.

The journey of a thousand miles (or marathons) is all about the journey

What would you estimate to be the number of people who give up on their dreams each day, week and year? I suspect a lot, and for a multitude of assumed reasons. Some reasons may be valid, to a point, but I often wonder how little importance such dreams may have had for the dreamer to fully give up.

I've learned to check in on my own desires for the future on a daily basis and to adjust them according to how my life changes over time. Rock climbs that I once aspired to ascend in my teenage years are now far too difficult and dangerous for me. But I can still enjoy the same pleasures of moving vertically and feeling the thrill of a potential fall, even if it is a fall that holds little risk of injury. One of my best friends wanted to be a professional football player but had his dreams squashed by an early injury that took too many years to recover from. He later became one of the world's leading experts in sports injuries and gets to connect with some of the world's best football players, while being an essential part of many teams. He also still delights in a kick-around with his local amateur team every month. We can each participate now in what our dreams hold for us, or once held for us. There can be few sadder or crazier ideas than that of missing the now for what may, or may not, come in the future, or giving up entirely and not appreciating some degree of what we want. If you take a long, slow look around you, you will see that 'now' is the only time we truly have, so isn't it sensible to live it as fully as it can be lived?

Mike: 'Please ask him.'
Translator: 'It is disrespectful.'
Mike: 'Really? I don't think so. It's not meant to be disrespectful, I am just very curious.'

Our Japanese translator bowed deeply as she asked the question of Gyosho Uehara, the 'Daigyoman Ajari' – or 'Saintly Master of the Highest Practice'.

Translator: (To Gyosho) 'He asks: would you do it again?'

Much to her relief, he smiled and replied in an enthusiastic and light tone.

Translator: 'He says that you are thinking about Kaihogyo [the act of running around the mountain for 100, 300 or 1,000 days] in the wrong way. He experienced enlightenment many days before completing this task. But finishing is not the goal, because there is no goal except being present to all that is happening.'

Coming from the holiest man in Japan, who trotted out daily marathons for a continuous 100, 300 and then 1,000 days around an often treacherous mountain and who sat through seven days of no sleep, food or water, I think that is pretty good advice: be present to each moment and appreciate the journey, not only the outcome.

CHAPTER 9

FREEDOM TO BE OURSELVES

The subjects of meditation and simplifying our physical world are in this last chapter not to present a world-view or model of how to live, but rather to highlight a thread that runs throughout this book: our experiences are internal and therefore the more choice we have over our internal states, the less we are dependent upon external complexity.

> *'There is only one success: to be able to spend your life in your own way.'*
>
> Christopher Morley, American journalist and poet

RIP

Life ran out. You just died. My condolences.

You float down a long tunnel towards a bright light. You arrive, to be proven incorrect/correct (believers may feel smug watching the atheists and agnostics look concerned about what comes next) about a physically located planet/country/floating island/fun park called 'heaven'. You saunter towards the gates to see a sign 'closed for repairs'. A voice booms out at you, 'Not today, kiddo, go back down the tunnel until we've fixed the plumbing.' You return to life and as you do, you get to experience all of the events of your earthly years in lightning replay speed.

As you open your eyes you have a profound realisation: all of the valuable moments in your life were when you ... (note down your thoughts in your notebook/journal or in the space provided below).

_____

_____

_____

In the previous chapter, I proposed the importance of understanding what qualities our dreams contain so that we can begin living elements of them straight away.

I invite you to add to what might be missing in your present life, by asking,

'If you really were to be at the end of your life now, looking back, what would you regret not having said and done?'

_____

_____

_____

_____

_____

The answers to this last question may help you answer another important question of this book: How do you specify what a good life means to you?

_____

_____

_____

There are many theories regarding what we humans need to become fulfilled and achieve optimum experiences.

All the way back in 1943, the American psychologist, Abraham Maslow, released a paper on 'A theory of human motivation', in which he presented the idea that humans can move through different stages of psychological growth that could culminate in what he termed 'self-actualisation'. Maslow described self-actualisation as 'the desire to accomplish everything that one can, to become the most that one can be'.

Most presentations of Maslow's theory are pictured in a pyramid, such as in the diagram below (though apparently, Maslow himself never used the pyramid model), which gives the impression of an upwardly sequential gain in achieving the various elements presented.

SELF-ACTUALISATION
morality, creativity, spontaneity, acceptance, purpose, meaning and inner potential

SELF-ESTEEM
confidence, achievement, respect of others, the need to be a unique individual

LOVE AND BELONGING
friendship, family, intimacy, sense of connection

SAFETY AND SECURITY
health, employment, property, family and social ability

PHYSIOLOGICAL NEEDS
breathing, food, water, shelter, clothing, sleep

To research his theory, Maslow studied 'exemplary people', or what we might now call 'models of excellence', such as Albert Einstein and Eleanor Roosevelt, along with studying the top one per cent of healthy college students at the time. The hierarchy that resulted from his studies points towards an obvious need (for most) to first attain the basics of life, such as air, food, water, shelter and clothing, before then moving up through next-level needs such as safety and security, through to love and belonging, self-esteem and finally the alleged ultimate of self-actualisation.

What you may already have noticed about Maslow's model is that beyond the very obvious essential survival needs for air, food, water, shelter and rest, everything else that he points at is an experience of varying degrees of non-survival-related states. All of the other experiences that are presented as equally essential are simply versions of how we feel, because when you think about it from a wider, holistic view, everything we are motivated to do is done so that we can feel in certain ways.

It could be that you choose to achieve the states proposed by Maslow by travelling to foreign countries, supporting causes, building businesses, joining clubs, dating/getting married, studying, inventing, making art, teaching, playing team sports, parenting, running marathons, writing books, climbing mountains, meditating or pretty much any activity that you engage in a (self-assigned and self-defined) meaningful way. Simply by changing the context we inhabit, the options for creating different feelings become endless. Though with practice, it is also possible to experience those same states simply by recalling them and fully associating to what you see and hear in a hallucinated and recalled version of events. To be able to do so is really useful when you find yourself engaging in some unresourceful activity next time – say impulse shopping. Rather than parting with your hard-earned money you could just recall what it feels like to buy a similar item, followed by the dull normalness of the item having lost its appeal some days later. I mention Maslow's hierarchy because it is a model that is quoted a lot and it represents the idea that there are specific needs that require meeting for us to be happy, content or whatever your idea of a good life requires.

So let us imagine, for a moment, what a self-actualised human having reached his or her potential might actually experience. I would assume such a person to be in perfect health, with glowing skin and sparkling teeth as a consequence of her complete self-awareness regarding which lifestyle habits provide maximum energy and health. Her posture would be straight and balanced, without excess tension anywhere in her musculature system. During rest she would have deep, even breathing, and when confronted by potential stress, she would re-access that deep breathing in a split second.

This wonder-woman, at the pinnacle of human development, would be successful on her own terms, working at what she finds to be most worthy of her skills each day. Her friends and family would love her for the way she seamlessly changed her range of emotions to fit the context. She would be congru- ently confident in her own abilities, while also being humble enough to remain open and curious about everything of which she had no direct experience. She would live by her own set of ethics, be endlessly compassionate, honest, creative and ever-present and engaged in the world around her, even when she removed herself from the world to contemplate her existence.

In all aspects of this imagined, realised human's life she would be operating from highly resourceful states and have choice available to her in everything she did. That sounds good, doesn't it?

I appreciate Maslow's concept of living towards a set of optimum states, but also view it as just that – a concept. The practicalities of achieving and accomplishing 'everything we can be' contains an inherent assumption that there is a peak, or limit, to our potential. If we became fully self-actualised, what else would we learn about life? More so, how could we ever make new choices? Which, if you consider what your own best life might be, almost certainly contains a deepening of choices in what matters most to you. This book, if you have not already worked it out, is written to enable you in the creation of choices, by interrupting and swapping your un-useful patterns or non-choices for more useful options. In essence, it is a swap of the poor neurological processes we wrap up in the name of ideas, beliefs, values, states and behaviours, all picked up over our lifetime of activity. Ideas, beliefs, values, states and behaviours drive our lives every day and mostly in ways we do not even recognise, because they remain unconscious to us. But what we can, and often do, recognise are the effects on our lives from how we interact with the world.

Unlike Maslow's idea of the actualised human who is required to move through additional experiences to achieve ultimate states, it could be that the really important states already exist in us as a natural norm. It's what we learn and pick up along the way that stimulates the feelings and behaviours we would rather be without. Under that baggage could well exist all of the positive states and resourcefulness we could ever want. It may simply be that we do not commit enough time and focus to stripping back our learned behaviours and creating the freedom to be ourselves.

Mr Happy

'The mind is malleable. Our life can be greatly transformed by even a minimal change in how we manage our thoughts and perceive and interpret the world. Happiness is a skill. It requires effort and time.'

It could be worth taking note of these words. They were spoken in an interview with M. Matthieu Ricard, a French biochemist turned Buddhist monk, who was given the title 'the world's happiest man' by researchers at the University of Wisconsin.

A paper published in 2004 opened the eyes of neuroscientists to the connection between meditation and happiness. Cognitive scientist Dr Richard Davis placed 128 electrodes on Ricard's head and monitored brain activity as he meditated upon unconditional love and kindness. The resulting brain scans showed extraordinarily high gamma waves, which only arise during intensely focused thought, at levels far beyond what the majority of us experience each day.

The same experiment was repeated with another group of meditators consisting of eight monks with between 10,000 to 50,000 hours of meditation practice, and a control group of university students with no meditation experience at all. Similar results were recorded. The monks produced 30 times more gamma waves than the student control group and much larger areas of the monks' brains became activated while meditating, particularly in the left prefrontal cortex, the area of the brain that is dominant when experiencing positive emotions.

Meditators, or 'mind-trainers' for those who have an aversion to anything 'spiritual sounding', are generally happier than regular folks and seem to have an increased base line of positive states that they experience throughout the day.

There are many likely reasons for this increased degree of happiness, ranging from electro/chemical alterations, the effects of discipline, decreasing the amount of mental activity and many other elements that may, as yet, be outside our range of understanding. What you will likely appreciate if you experience 10 minutes of daily meditation is that when we bring all of our attention back to breath and physiology, there are sometimes blissful moments of freedom from all the usual chatter, considerations and internal activity. We get to experience our little reality as simply and elegantly as can be, while our usual maps of subjective reality rest a while. By experiencing these 'map-free' states, even for only a few minutes, we get to know directly how heavily many of our more common states weigh upon us, as well as having an alternative experience that comes without our usual beliefs, values and ways of interpreting our world.

This last point is really important if you are someone who has a tightly limited view of the world, because after experiencing a know-nothing state you can use it to provide a retrospective glimpse into what your pre-conditioned, un-trained selves were like, before you took on all of your current programming concerning reality. When we have no internal chatter or self-awareness, only a pleasant total experience, we are essentially disproving much of what we believe to be true about reality, namely that our version of it is THE version of it.

In a way, meditating is a little re-set that clears our neurology from the excesses we place upon it. And it would seem that the more we remove, the more our base line of experience becomes naturally pleasant.

Goodbye self

Among many Eastern traditions, the concept of 'enlightenment' generally seems to mean the loss of all ego, including any notion of personal identity from extended periods of no self-talk. In place of the ever-questioning, judging, monkey-mind and conditioned reactions to the world is an alleged state of happiness, bliss and contentment. To attain these levels of peak-state apparently requires many years of dedicated practice, be it running around a Japanese mountain or sitting straight-backed and directing all attention towards the breath as a way to subdue thoughts that might otherwise lead the practitioner away from each present moment.

Most of the yogic/meditation practices aim to reduce cravings and desires, and aversions and loathing. Allegedly, somewhere in the middle of not wanting and not avoiding there exists a perfect state of contentment, the consequence of which seems to be a base line of enjoyable states.

There are thousands of years of evidence for the benefits of these inner-type approaches. If you look at history, it would seem that very few people from the cultures that regularly meditate go on to become crusaders or terrorists in a bid to push their particular belief system on the world. I know from my own experiences that this is partly because the practice creates such relaxed, content and peaceful states that even hurting a fly has the effect of altering our awareness in an unacceptable form.

There is also very little likelihood of forcing a process of constant attention to our breath and physiology onto a mass of non-practitioners.

Personally, what compels me the most to sit cross-legged for 10 minutes each day are the states of deep relaxation during meditation, and for some time afterwards, which by experiencing even for a minute, loads those states into my nervous system library for later recall anytime I choose to be at my most relaxed.

If you have meditated before, you can do this too, right now, by remembering what it feels like to be in the meditation state, along with relaxing your sight into peripheral vision, dropping your tongue down and forward so that it doesn't move, and shifting your breath and posture into a tension-free setting. Regardless of where you are or what you're experiencing in your environment, you can easily access a state of meditation-like relaxation with these steps.

If you have never meditated before, the same steps will help you begin training your neurology to go into a relaxed state, something more and more people are finding difficult to do with the constant stimulation of smartphones and always being connected.

PATTERN:

Steps to achieve a meditation-like state

1. Scan your body for tension and release it where you find it.
2. Breathe a little deeper into the belly, without forcing it, and slow your breath down.
3. Focus on one spot ahead of you and then, while staying focused, begin to broaden your field of view into peripheral vision, so that you are taking in everything above, below and to the sides of the one spot that you are focusing upon.
4. Drop your tongue down and forward just below your gums. Place just enough pressure on the gum line so that your tongue does not move. By stopping the tiny muscle movements of the tongue, our internal self-talk magically ceases.

More ritualistic meditation techniques vary as widely as the cultures that have utilised them. There are literally hundreds of differing patterns to achieve the know-nothing states as can be seen if you put 'meditation' into any online book store.

In much of the literature on meditation, the outcome often seems aimed towards achieving states of happiness and contentment. I suspect that few of us would turn down the chance to experience 30 times more gamma waves if we could actually appreciate what that means. But few of us have the time or space to sit for many hours a day and do nothing except rearrange our internal software. And of all the states that we experience, happiness may be the most elusive. It is often triggered by rare and unexpected events and can also be confused with experiences of satisfaction, or love or some other state that really cannot be accurately labelled. If it was even possible to label any state accurately at all.

It is important to remember that the states we experience consciously and label as 'happy', 'sad', or whatever, are signals from the primitive parts of our neurology and that to override all unwanted signals with permanent happiness would be dangerous. Happiness is the last feeling you want when your unconscious is urging you to walk away from the danger that is brewing in a bar, or when someone is lying to you to get what he or she wants. Similarly, when we experience seeing other people suffer, happiness is far from appropriate as it is unlikely to compel us to take action to relieve that suffering.

As with everything on offer in this book, the states that we might aim to experience from any activity, including practices such as meditation, should always be a choice. I suspect that the world's happiest person can switch on the bliss pretty quickly, while also being able to switch to another state so he or she can experience the world through equally useful filters.

Simplify

'The more you know the less you need.'

Aboriginal saying

Meditation is one path of many for experiencing the freedom to be ourselves, if what I am calling 'freedom' is to be without all, or some of, our conditioned responses. When you consider how we engage in so many other activities to experience states of some kind or other (some people jump out of aeroplanes, some collect stamps, some eat food, some collect wives/husbands, some shoot guns, some …), there is certainly an elegance and simplicity in sitting and just being present to our breath and posture. Just 10 minutes a day is hardly a lot to ask of even the busiest individuals, who by being so busy likely need the time-out most of all to consciously connect with the sensations running within them.

Simplicity seems to be a condition that when acted upon, or rather, not acted upon, can have the effect of supporting many positive experiences, whether we meditate for 10,000 hours or not.

As our world becomes ever more complex and demanding by the day, it is clear to see how so many people struggle with keeping resourceful, optimum states. Attention-grabbing events, devices and to-do lists are so far beyond what our neurology evolved to be able to handle that we are now living in entirely uncharted territory regarding the potential long-term effects. The ability to dissociate from the experience of stressful events and overload could well be the most important patterns to teach our kids in future generations. When a person can dissociate from outside events they are free to choose how to respond, rather than what we see now in the form of endless individuals suffering from chronic stress, or what I'd more correctly term, lack of choice. And even with a full dissociation to everyday stress, our lives still require attending to, meaning that, no matter how relaxed or 'Zen' we are, things still have to get done.

For many busy people, this becomes a matter of getting more organised and automated, while missing a parallel solution of streamlining life so that there is less to be done in the first place.

Have you ever daydreamed of living in a tropical beach hut, sleeping in a hammock and watching the sea lap against the shore, or simply wondered how much you could reduce complicatedness while still functioning effectively in the world? Do you remember from the last chapter that I suggested that our dreams contain the qualities of what we are not currently experiencing?

Two of my good friends dreamed often of having less complicated lives and then went after those dreams in the present. Ryan and Mel experimented with reducing their physical stuff and responsibilities to the barest minimum for one year or until they really could not live without their objects any longer. This included only using certain apps on their smartphones for an hour per day and only sending emails from their work locations. They packed up somewhere in the region of 40 boxes of clothes and household stuff and retained just enough clothing for one week without washing, along with three cups, forks, knives, spoons and plates. Ryan packed up all his books, CDs and gaming devices but was certain he would be pulling them out again after only a week or so.

Ryan is a coach, who knows how to change his states regardless of what is going on around him, and Mel is an artist and creative. Their intention for simplifying was to test the theory that it would give them more time together and support Mel's creative needs. What actually happened was an experience that seems to be common among people who make changes to their lives by reducing the amount of objects and commitments they have. It took only the first month for them to become hooked on their new lifestyle choice of minimalism, and as they are now in their third year of living with minimum belongings, they make it an ongoing focus to simplify more and more.

In that first month, Mel and Ryan experienced a range of benefits from living without the trappings of their former life, including:

- They began saving money because their rule was to buy nothing that was not absolutely essential.
- They had more time for family and friends.
- Ryan started writing his book.
- They ate out less and cooked at home, which improved their health.
- They read books and had long conversations most nights because there was no TV or Internet at home.
- They both experienced fewer distractions.
- Both of them spent more time engaging in activities they enjoyed, rather than cruising the net and watching TV.
- Their energy levels improved as they experienced less stress.
- They felt more 'connected' with each other.
- Mel's creative output increased.

This last effect (Mel's increased creativity) is really an example of what I regard as most important about simplifying as much of our lives as we can. Our conscious mind only has enough attention for a limited amount of stimulation and when we live in an environment of excess stuff, digital connection and endless media, we spend much of our time reacting instead of thinking, creating and experiencing what is worthwhile to us.

I personally have no moral or value-based judgement around having lots of stuff (though that may change as we slip further into environmental challenges). The reason I offer the process of simplifying is because most of us are now living insanely complex and busy lives that would almost certainly benefit from having fewer distractions rather than more.

A home full of bulging cupboards and piles of bills, a diary so full that there is no time to eat during the day, an inbox and phone that contain hundreds of messages screaming for attention. All of these challenges can be experienced by us in a state of stress, anxiety and fear – or engaged with in a relaxed, resourceful state that enables us to get more done and with fewer undesirable consequences.

Training our neurology to respond resourcefully, regardless of the context, is the important lesson of this book. With practice of the patterns offered so far, anyone can become adept at doing so. So the obvious question is, once we are able to respond in a useful way, why would we even concern ourselves with simplicity on the outside, if we have everything in order on the inside? I regard it as 'having the best of both worlds'.

Some benefits that might arise from simplifying your life:

1. Time: Let's assume you stopped allocating whole afternoons to shopping for more stuff. Learned to say 'no' to all of the people who do not enrich your experiences. You have reduced your time on social media and reading about other people's lives. You have given your TV to the local charity shop and you no longer use up hours of time cleaning, washing and ironing excess clothes. Once-bulging cupboards are now neatly ordered and after a brief period of reduction, many of your previous time-consuming distractions have disappeared. The consequence? You now have time to engage in the most meaningful/fun/rewarding ways you see fit. Though, admittedly, some folks find that shopping, TV, cleaning clothes and tidying cupboards are THE most meaningful/fun/rewarding pastimes in their life!

2. Contentment: When we shift our perspective so that minimising is a positive process that we actively seek, we liberate our thoughts from discontented, 'I can't afford that', or 'I really want one of those but it's out of my range' to 'I have a relatively new car already. What am I going to do with a vintage Aston Martin, except worry

about scratching it while parking in the city?' By adopting a minimalist attitude, you alter your thinking time regarding spending money, as well as conserving energy on the accumulation process.

3. 'Healthy people have many wishes, the sick have only one.' If there is one condition that all health experts agree upon it is that excess stress, regardless of the source, can affect our health negatively. Stress is a broad term for a range of triggers that can provoke inflammatory responses in our system and, in fact, from the moment we are born, we are 'stressed' from multiple sources in our environment. What enables us to positively respond to stress by reducing inflammation, repairing, reproducing and detoxifying our organs as well as allowing our immunity to flourish, is that freely available gift of restoration we call 'sleep'.

In certain circles, there seems to be a competitive approach to who can survive on the least sleep and get the greatest amount of work done. I don't get it. I have worked with a number of insomniacs over the years and all of them experience miserable daytime lows and trouble with attention and motivation. I can appreciate the equation that the more sleep we get, the less waking time we have. But who cares about a few extra hours if you feel like crap all day? If you are not waking up full of beans, feeling rested, hungry and ready for the day, you need more sleep. If we cut the late-night sessions of Internet, TV, texting and bar-crawling and get an extra hour or two of quality sleep, the knock-on effect in our daytime activities is worth more than a hundred espressos.

4. Discover more. There's a big world out there just waiting for your discovery. Likewise, there is a big world inside of you, waiting for even more discovery. When we are not focused on consumption and accumulation as dominant activities, we can create the space to answer better questions, such as what's really important to us, what are our missions, what are our true passions, and maybe even how can we contribute to making positive changes in our world.

We all need ample amounts of Maslow's base motivations: food, shelter, clothing, health care, etc. However, beyond a certain point of attainment, it seems that many people experience reduced benefits from all their efforts to have more and more.

For instance, a study by the economist Angus Deaton and psychologist Daniel Kahneman found that $75,000 of yearly earnings seemed to be the point where people experienced a degree of happiness and contentment that levelled out and *did not* increase with higher earnings. When people earned above that amount, the difference they experienced was a sense of life working out better for them. However, no increase in happiness was noted, regardless of increase in earnings.

If you consider the difference in living standards between a family living on $20,000 a year and one on $75,000, the results are dramatic. But going from $75,000 to many millions does not seem to have a notable effect on happiness and contentment. Maybe it's a bit like the first cold drink you have on a hot, sunny day. None of the subsequent drinks have anywhere near the same satisfying effect. In fact, if that drink is a beer, as we drink more and more, the effects ultimately get worse and, in the end, even the most hard-livered types have to stop and pay some form of attention to what they are experiencing.

Do it for you, not them

I invite you to engage in a little fantasy … You wake up tomorrow with all of your material needs met, along with all of the approval (should you be foolish enough to seek such responses from others) you believe you require. You never again need to work for money or acceptance.

What do you do?

If you can answer this question honestly you will get a clearer appreciation of what you value and how close or far you are to living aligned with what is important to you.

This little excursion into fantasy is not designed to get you thinking about life with unlimited money and rhino-thick skin. It is to alert you to how we make decisions based upon financial factors and what we assume other people may think of us, meaning 'mind-reading', which as you know, is a skill that none of us is likely to possess.

You probably know of people who seem to live their lives attempting to impress you and others, but it is rare that 'impressing' ever takes place. In fact, the opposite is mostly true as even the most unobservant of us can attest. We easily spot the difference between the person who is hoping to impress and the person who is genuinely impressive.

Making choices based on status and the approval of others is like handing over the steering wheel of your life. We can never control the full opinion of others because we will never be able to locate ourselves in their brain and shift all of their values to fit those we are attempting to impress.

But even if you do manage to impress others with a display of wealth, intelligence and prestige, what next?

Who next?

You can be a king or a pauper, and yet, sitting for minutes and focusing on your breath, or running wild with the wind in your hair, or dancing with a loved one to the music of your youth will provide a break in experience so that you are neither. You can be surrounded by extreme wealth or extreme poverty, but if you know how to choose your states, your environment matters little. For some, reducing the obsession with stuff and mundane activities, along with reducing negative thoughts, may well be so rewarding because it brings us back to the simple fact that everything 'out there' is only as relevant, valid, meaningful or meaningless as who or what 'in here' chooses it to be.

You may long to surround yourself with beauty, nature, art and functionality when you can, just do not allow such things, or their absence, to determine how you feel. Every minute you waste on experiencing unpleasant, un-resourceful states represents 60 seconds you could spend being happy, joyful, appreciative, excited, resourceful and making the very most of our most limited commodities – our time.

What is the real cost of it?

Time is the leveller that has no bias or regard for beliefs, status, rank or race. Each of us has the same number of hours to use in every day, with no special benefits added to our clocks for working harder or being smarter. Tick tock – it is the same countdown for each of us.

Some people are smarter than others and will maximise their biology in the hope of extending the life in their veins. If you drink, smoke and eat processed foods each day you cannot really complain about the potential for checking out of life a few decades earlier than your healthier living counterparts. Likewise, jumping off cliffs and kissing crocodiles adds to the possibility of reducing time in the game.

Time as the one absolute of life is also the one equal currency that we all have to trade each day, and as Henry David Thoreau pointed out:

> 'The cost of a thing is the amount of what I will call life which is required to be exchanged for it, immediately or in the long run.'

Thoreau's definition of 'life' could mean energy expended, and almost certainly means time required to attain that 'thing'.

Over a lifetime of 80 years our usage of time can be far from what we assume.

- Watching the average of 2.5 hours of TV from the age of four means that you lose 7.5 full, around the clock, years of life staring at a box of moving pictures.
- Spending 8 hours a week in a bar loses you a cool, continual 2 years of life.
- Being employed full-time from the age of 21 means that, 12 years, or more, of 24 hours a day were spent fully at work.
- Commuters taking 1.5 hours each day lose another 2 years.
- Four years of total life is now estimated to be the time spent using our smartphones. Four years!?
- Seven hours of sleep per night takes up 25 years, which totals these activities to 52.5 years, to leave ... 27.5 or so years in which you have the chance to really 'live'.

How much of that 27.5 years, if we actually make it to 80 years of age, is spent worrying, stressing, arguing, convalescing, fighting, gossiping, hating, envying, procrastinating ... and going through life with hardly a whiff of curiosity, adventure, contentment, love, joy and happiness?

Tick tock, tick tock ...

However it's also valuable not to conflate clock time with time experienced.

When you were last in the company of a trusted and beloved friend or family member, how did time move for you – who did you think of and how long did it take?

When making love, how much relevance does clock time have?

When you were swept up in a great novel or movie, could you hear the seconds ticking?

Each of us experiences time distortion coming from our altered states, whether induced by boredom and drudgery, being in love or loving what we are doing.

I could not really tell you how long it has taken me to fall down the entire length of a cliff face and still survive on one of my luckier days as a climber.

If you are a mother, you will know how much time you experienced in the various stages of birthing your child and how little relevance the clock had.

When I listen to my sons' laughter, it echoes down my neurological pathways over and over, while all of time stands still for me.

Though many cultures impose it, there is nothing forcing us to live by clock time, and if we do, it is because we have become hopeless slaves of a socially imposed construct. There are plenty of people around who are slaves of time – it is easy to identify them by looking at their wrists, or better still, just asking them whether they are hungry and then noticing if they look at their watch to decide, as opposed to connecting to their body sensations.

Time is certainly limited at some point for all of us, but what is important is how we live our lives, in what states we choose to approach each day, how open we are to the strangeness, the differences and the beauty of our world. How do you choose to live with dignity today, even as you work for tomorrow? Will you step outside of yourself each day and observe how you are really living, and in the process give attention to the bigger questions of your life? Will you even question everything you believed to be true and continue to question it even as new answers arise?

Could you, like the great stoics, live with nothing or face your worst fears, while knowing that everything you hold on to and reject is simply your own reality tunnel at play?

There are multiple new worlds waiting for us, right there in front of our eyes. All it takes is to un-train our inner relationship to our outer world, and be open to embrace new experiences as we go about readying ourselves for an adventure or two. As Mark Twain suggested:

> *'Twenty years from now you will be more disappointed by the things that you didn't do than by the ones you did do.*
>
> *So throw off the bowlines.*
>
> *Sail away from the safe harbour.*
>
> *Catch the trade winds in your sails.*
>
> *Explore.*
>
> *Dream.*
>
> *Discover.'*

And I would add, 'be free'.

APPENDICES

Acknowledgements, further reading and references

Pattern credits

The patterns in this book have been modelled and developed from the behaviours and attitudes of world-class individuals, providing a code of how those individuals do what they do.

The original developers of these patterns are as follows:

The five-step change process (known in Neuro Linguistic Programming or NLP as the New Code Change Format), John Grinder with later variations by Carmen Bostic St. Clair

Perceptual positions had two strong antecedent sources. What is now coded as 'Third Position' was called 'meta position' in the classic code of NLP.

The second antecedent was Gregory Bateson's double description – from *Steps to an Ecology of Mind*. Judith Delozier participated in the connection that led from Bateson's double description to what later was developed into the current code by Carmen Bostic St. Clair.

Rhythm of life, Breath of life, Peripheral ball game and Chain of excellence (breath influences physiology, influences state, influences behaviour), John Grinder and Carmen Bostic St. Clair

The Intention/consequence pattern used throughout this book, Carmen Bostic St. Clair

Unconscious signals, also known as 'the breakthrough pattern', and sway pattern, John Grinder

Complex equivalence from 'the meta model' developed by John Grinder and Richard Bandler

Alphabet game – The original format was a mix of Roger Tabb and John Grinder, with later variations by Carmen Bostic St. Clair

Recommended reading

Bandler, Richard and John Grinder, *The Structure of Magic*, volume 1 (Science and Behaviour Books, 1975)

Bateson, Gregory, *Mind and Nature: A Necessary Unity* (E.P. Dutton, 1979)

Bateson, Gregory, *Steps to an Ecology of Mind* (Ballantine Books, 1972)

Bostic St. Clair, Carmen and John Grinder, *Whispering in the Wind* (J. & C. Enterprises, 2001)

McGilchrist, Iain, *The Master and his Emissary* (Yale University Press, 2009)

Pierce, J. Howard, *The Owner's Manual for the Brain* (Bard Press, 2006)

Rasmussen, Jorgen, *Provocative Hypnosis: The No Holds Barred Interventions of a Contrarian Change Artist* (2008)

Thoreau, Henry David, *Walden and Civil Disobedience* (*Walden* first published by Ticknor and Fields, 1854; *Civil Disobedience* first published 1849)

Wilson, Robert Anton, *Prometheus Rising* (New Falcon Publications, 1983)

References

The breast crawl: http://www.breastcrawl.org/science.shtml

Mirror neurons were first discovered in the pre-motor area F5 of macaque monkeys (di Pellegrino et al., 1992; Gallese et al., 1996; Rizzolatti et al., 2001; Umiltà et al., 2001)

Thereafter they were found in the inferior parietal lobule, area PF (Gallese et al., 2002; Fogassi et al., 2005).

Alhola, Paula and Päivi Polo-Kantola, 'Sleep deprivation: Impact on cognitive performance', Sleep Research Unit, Department of Physiology, University of Turku, Finland

Berkman L.F., Syme S.L., 'Social networks, host resistance, and mortality: a nine-year follow-up study of Alameda County residents'

Gardner, Martha N., Phd and Allan M. Brandt, PhD, 'The Doctors' Choice is America's Choice: The Physician in US Cigarette Advertisements, 1930–1953'

Giltay E.J., Geleijnse J.M., Zitman F.G., Hoekstra T., Schouten E.G., 'Dispositional optimism and all-cause and cardiovascular mortality in a prospective cohort of elderly Dutch men and women', Psychiatric Center GGZ Delfland, Delft; Division of Human Nutrition, Wageningen University, Wageningen, the Netherlands

Kahneman, Daniel and Angus Deaton, 'High income improves evaluation of life but not emotional well-being', Center for Health and Well-being, Princeton University, Princeton, NJ 08544

Maruta T., Colligan R.C., Malinchoc M., Offord K.P., 'Optimism-pessimism assessed in the 1960s and self-reported health status 30 years later', Department of Psychiatry and Psychology, Mayo Clinic, Rochester, Minn 55905

Ramachandran: the neurons that shaped civilization (TED Talk): https://www.ted.com/talks/vs_ramachandran_the_neurons_that_shaped_civilization?language=en

Stanovich, Keith E., Richard F. West, Maggie E. Toplak, 'Myside Bias, Rational Thinking, and Intelligence', *Current Directions in Psychological Science*, August 2013, vol. 22 no. 4, 259–64

Meditation: http://www.matthieuricard.org/en/articles/categories/articles-about-science

Work with me

If you'd like to learn more about the author, be coached or train with him, please go to: www.mikeweeks.co

For video and audio of all the patterns in this book, along with many more ways to un-train your brain: www.untrainyourbrain.com

Special thanks

Who knew that writing a book was a team sport!

I wish to make special thanks to the following people:

Dr M. Amir, the world-famous Putney dentist, who reached out to Vermilion to get this book underway.

Joanne Dixon and Olga Petreanu, who are my life support in my many ventures away from writing.

My agent, Robert Kirby at United Talent for his deal-making acumen whilst being a really decent human.

My dear friend and 'fourth position', Daryll Scott, who I hope will continue to be as generous with his genius support in all my future projects.

Jorgen Rasmussen for inspiring more creative ways to generate change.

Pedro Noya for his trust, friendship and patience whilst waiting for me to finish this book.

To James Thorpe and Jessica Kelly for their differing, and yet hugely enjoyable efforts to spur me on.

Chris Thompkins for allowing me to ride with him into the heat and be a regular part of www.clarionglobalresponse.org

My editing team:

Extra special thanks go to my close friend and first editor, Sunita Toor, who spent countless hours questioning my writing and ensuring that I didn't get lost in my own hubris.

Christiane Haberl for the Austrian touch.

Jo Godfrey Wood for swooping in at the eleventh hour and pushing for clarity.

Sam Jackson at Vermilion, who expected more from me and
then managed to get it whilst remaining patient and com-
posed like the pro she is.

To John Grinder and Carmen Bostic St. Clair for giving me legs
to run before the wind.

To all of the people I have worked with around the world, and
who I will continue to share inner and outer adventures with
in the quest to live freer lives.

To Bean Sopwith, my wife, best friend and greatest teacher of all.

QR code URLs

Page 24: The body scan
http://untrainyourbrain.com/videos/The-body-scan

Page 37: Making states
http://untrainyourbrain.com/videos/State-shifter

Page 44: Perceptual positions
http://untrainyourbrain.com/videos/Perceptual-positions-1-2-3

Page 54: Cause/effect
http://untrainyourbrain.com/videos/Cause-Effect

Page 110: Unconscious signals
http://untrainyourbrain.com/videos/Unconscious-signals

Page 111: Creating an ally
http://untrainyourbrain.com/videos/Creating-an-Ally

Page 113: Sway pattern
http://untrainyourbrain.com/videos/The-Sway-pattern

Page 124: State transfer
http://untrainyourbrain.com/videos/State-Transfer

Page 128: Breathe and ripple
http://untrainyourbrain.com/videos/Breathe-and-ripple

Page 139: Second position
http://untrainyourbrain.com/videos/2nd-position

Page 150: Looking back from the future
http://untrainyourbrain.com/videos/Looking-back-from-
the-future

Page 168: Rhythm of life
http://untrainyourbrain.com/videos/The-rhythm-of-life

Page 172: Memory engineering
http://untrainyourbrain.com/videos/Memory-engineering

Page 192: Intention/consequence
http://untrainyourbrain.com/videos/Intention-Consequence

Page 198: Peripheral ball game
http://untrainyourbrain.com/videos/Peripheral-vision-ball-game

Page 205: Alphabet game
http://untrainyourbrain.com/videos/The-Alphabet-Game

Page 217: Meditation states
http://untrainyourbrain.com/videos/Meditation-states

INDEX